The Immigrant Boy

A Townsville Boyhood – 1912-1918

Marion Houldsworth

The Clark Family, 1917, settled and prospering.

National Library of Australia Cataloguing-in-Publication entry
Author: Houldsworth, Marion.
Title: The immigrant boy / Marion Houldsworth.
ISBN: 9781921920974 (pbk.)
Subjects: Immigrants--Queensland--Townsville--Biography.
           British--Queensland--Townsville--Biography.
           Children of immigrants--Great Britain--Biography.
           Townsville (Qld.)--Social life and customs--20th century.
Dewey Number: 920.72

Typeset in Warnock Pro 12 pt.
Cover Design: Marion Houldsworth

Published by Boolarong Press, Salisbury, Brisbane, Australia.
Printed and bound by Watson Ferguson & Company, Salisbury, Brisbane, Australia.

About the Author

Marion Houldsworth was born in Mount Morgan, Central Queensland, and grew up in Western Queensland and Townsville. She was educated at Blackheath College, Charters Towers, Rockhampton Girls' Grammar School and the University of Queensland. Together with her husband she taught for many years in the Northern Territory and New Guinea.

Her previous published works include:

Hearts Bright with Hope; A Grammar School Diary

The Morning Side of the Hill; Growing up in Townsville in World War Two (Boolarong Press)

Barefoot through the Bindies; Growing Up in North Queensland in the Early 1900s (Boolarong Press)

From the Gulf to God Knows Where; Living in Australia's Outback; Volume One (Central Queensland University Press)

Maybe it'll Rain Tomorrow; Living in Australia's Outback (Boolarong Press)

Red Dust Rising; The Life of Cattleman Ray Fryer (Boolarong Press)

Another Beautiful Day; Blackheath & Thornburgh College; 90 Years On (Boolarong Press)

Contents

About the Author   V

Acknowledgements   IX

Dedication   XI

Foreword   XIII

Illustrations   XV

Introduction   XVII

Part 1

The Voyage Out – 1912 – *'And we Come to Townsville'*   3

The Newcomers – 1912 – *'Mangoes you'd Bump your Head on'*   13

Flinders Street – 1913 – *'She Was a Good Town!'*   29

The Sound Effects Boy – 1913 – *'Nearly Midnight Before We'd Finish'*   45

The Little Battler – 1913 – *'Anything to Make a Quid'*   59

The Water Joey – 1914 – *'Nippering on the Line'*   73

Meatworks Boy – 1914 – *'You Made Your Own Excitement'*   83

The Apprentice – 1914-1918 – *'I Learned to Love the Game'*   97

Part Two – Joe's Mates

Harry Pope   111

Henry Brown   114

Julius Mathieson   117

Florrie Toombs   121

John Walker   123

Appendix

1) List of passengers arriving on the *Limerick*   125

2) Immigration Nominee Form: Clark Family   126

3) Extract from Townsville Electoral Roll, 1915, showing 864, Elizabeth Eleanor Clark, Stanley Street   127

4) Extract from Clark Family Bible 129

5) Extracts from the North Queensland Register, April 1911 – The *Yongala* wreckage found at Palm Island 130

Bibliography 132

Acknowledgements

I wish to thank Mr and Mrs T.K. Rains of Herveys Range, for permission to publish Joe's story, and for the use of the two Clark family photographs; also Mr Russel Clark, Joe's nephew, for the use of family letters and Edward Houldsworth for pencil drawings, *Mangoes* and *Boxing Gloves*. Long-time Townsville friends, Ron & Beryl Quelch, were ever supportive. Pearl Mahony suggested the source of the photographs of the *Limerick*, and located details of the Clark family in the Brisbane Records Office. Professor Alistair Thomson of Monash University, read the typescript and suggested helpful fine-tuning. Thanks are due to Townsville City Council for a generous grant towards cost of publication. The late Emeritus Professor Brian Dalton, of James Cook University's School of History and Politics shared my interest and delight in Joe Clark's boyish picture of Townsville in the early years of the twentieth century.

Dedication

For

Pearl Mahony,

who also delights in the generations

that have gone before.

Queensland Worker's Cottage. 1908

Foreword

Migrant stories speak to a powerful collective memory. Australian families of non-Aboriginal descent all have migrant stories from a recent past, some forgotten, some passed on through succeeding generations, perhaps embroidered along the way, helping us to understand where we have come from. Joe Clark's story vividly evokes a migrant experience: the extraordinary experience of leaving England; arrival in a startling new world; struggling to make a life against the odds.

As an old man Joe recalls his boyhood with pinpoint detail and rich colour. You can hear the memories coming to life as he talks, as one story jogs another, and at times we are transported back with Joe: sound effects boy at the Stanley Theatre, walking along dusty, smelly Flinders Street; at work in the saw mill or on the railway.

Images from childhood and youth are often our strongest memories, closely linked to significant places and rites of passage. I myself remember a Townsville boyhood in the 1970s: scrambling with mates around the derelict fort at Kissing Point; the huge boulders of the rock-pool walls strewn along the road after Cyclone Althea; mopping up the blood of a friend who fell down Castle Hill on a school trip. Mine was a very different boyhood to that of Joe Clark, who went to work, aged twelve when his father died just after their arrival in Australia. Townsville school-kids of today who read Joe's story will relish his account of almost-familiar places, yet they will also discover the ways in which Townsville, and teenage lives, have changed dramatically over the century.

Oral history is always a double act. First of all, an interviewer 'from the University' got Joe talking and taped his memories. Almost twenty years later and with Joe no longer around, Marion Houldsworth has skilfully crafted Joe's recording into this narrative. I am sure Joe would be pleased with the result, and to have this chance to live on in our imaginations.

Professor Alistair Thomson

Monash University

Illustrations

Frontispiece *The Clark Family c. 1917*

Shipping notes. Townsville Daily Bulletin, *4 Sepember 1912.*

Chapter 1   The Voyage Out

Limerick. Greenwich Maritime Museum Collection.
Crossing the Line. Greenwich Maritime Museum Collection.

Chapter 2   The Newcomers

Castle Hill from the Pilot Station. James Cook University Collection.
Joseph Clark, Senior (died 1912). Mr & Mrs T. K. Rains' Collection.

Chapter 3   Flinders Street

Flinders Street East, 1913. James Cook University Collection.
Imperial Hotel. James Cook University Collection.

Chapter 4   The Sound Effects Boy

Central Flinders Street, 1912. James Cook University Collection.
Stanley Pictures, Lowth's Hotel. John Oxley Library.

Chapter 5   The Little Battler

Railway Station 1912. James Cook University Collection.
Railway Station under construction. James Cook University Collection.

Chapter 6   The Water Joey

Fettlers' Camp. James Cook University Collection.
Railway Pumpers. James Cook University Collection.

Chapter 7   Meatworks Boy

Alligator Creek Meatworks, 1917. John Oxley Library.
Ross River Meatworks, 1917. John Oxley Library.

Chapter 8   The Apprentice

Cattle train from the West. John Oxley Library.
Coal Loading, Townsville Railway Yards. John Oxley Library.

Part 2 – Joe's Mates

Harry Pope – *Billy-goat cart*

Henry Brown – *Tent Home.*

Julius Mathieson – *Ruin of Pozières Windmill. Wikimedia Commons.*

Florrie Toombs– *Townsville Orphanage, ca. 1900s.*

John Walker– *Australian A.I.F. Rising Sun Badge Encampment, Kissing Point, Townsville, ca.1914. City Libraries Townsville.*

Introduction

I never met Joe Clark, and yet I feel I know him well. Joe's story was one of nearly nine hundred life histories in the archive of the North Queensland Oral History Project at James Cook University, Townsville. This project, commenced in the early 1970s, was originally funded by the Australian Research Council and aimed to record the life histories of North Queenslanders who were then in their eighties or over. I was searching this collection for material for a thesis on "Childhood in North Queensland at the Turn of the Twentieth Century" when I came across Joe Clark's story. Immediately it seemed to me that, half way between social history and a good yarn, his recollections merited publication for the graphic word-picture it gave of the Townsville of 1912 to 1918.

Most of the speakers on the audio-tapes of the North Queensland Oral History Archive begin the interview with a degree of reserved hesitancy. You can sense their thoughts: 'Someone from the University asking questions!' 'What sort of things are they going to ask?' 'S'posing it's something hard!' 'I'm not sure I like this'. But not so Joe Clark. 'Now!' the recording of his interview starts, 'I'm gunna be tellin' y'..', and sets about doing so at a cracking pace. You can almost see the interviewer startling back, with a 'Hey! What's going on! I'm supposed to be in charge here!'

But that was typical Joe. Joe Clark knew he had a life story worth telling, and he wanted to get on with it. Six tapes later he is still at it. In the meantime we have been borne backwards in time. Townsville is once more a small river port with streets of dirt, to cross which women must hold serge skirts above button-boots. Horse buses clip-clop past and Charlie Beale cracks his whip round the backsides of barefoot boys free-loading on the back step. The only other sound to be heard is the singing of the housemaids making up the beds on the pub verandahs. When the fire-bell rings in the tower next to the Post Office, volunteers pelt from all directions to help, and the horse-drawn engine gallops away in a cloud of dust. It is a small town of fewer than ten thousand people who live for the most part in weatherboard cottages around the mouth of Ross Creek.

Townsville had been established in the 1860s as a port for the pastoralists opening up the Kennedy District. Within a few years, the discovery of major goldfields in the hinterland, and the development of sugar-lands to the north and south boosted its development, until by the 1890s Townsville had outstripped its competitors, Bowen and Cardwell, and become the major outlet for the North, with a scattering of fine public buildings among the ubiquitous corrugated-iron shops and iron-lace verandahed hotels.

This was the Townsville to which the Clark family arrived on the immigrant ship, *Limerick,* on a bright September morning in 1912. The Interviewer neglected to ask, and Joe, not one to dwell overmuch on sentiment, does not tell us how the family, father, mother and four children, felt as they stood at the rail of the ship gazing at their new home across the shining waters of Cleveland Bay. Six weeks and twelve thousand miles distant from grey industrial Newcastle-on-Tyne they would have seen the sun glinting on tin roofs and the pink granite precipices of Castle Hill.

Fortunately for them they could bypass the Immigration Depot on Ross Island. They had relatives who had been their sponsors for the venture. Uncle James Arrowsmith lived in Stanley Street, and somewhere close by perhaps, he had rented a small weatherboard cottage for the new arrivals.

Joe is twelve years old, 'curious', as he tells us – 'if a boy's not curious there's something wrong with him' – and clearly beside himself with excitement. Everything he sees, and there is not much he misses, is strange and new: the coasters *Kuranda* and the *Mourilyan* in the Swing Basin, the *Clyde* the *Scout* and the *Lass o' Gowrie* further upstream against the busy wharves; the bullock-teams loading; Burns Philp's Store, which the local kids tell him is 'full of mouth-organs for the Kanakas'; a tin shed inside which, if you squinnied through the cracks, could be seen a 'stick and string' aeroplane which had mysteriously been 'dropped' on Ross River.

In notorious Flinders Lane there are Pakka-Pu and Fan Tan shops and opium dens. Chinamen with swinging pigtails jog around the weatherboard cottages with baskets of vegetables on bamboo poles. There are wild goats on the hill and plenty of others that roam the streets. There are strange new fruits: custard-apples, paw-paws, and mangoes 'you could bump your head on'. (Joe is no artist with words, except technical terms, but what a perfect description of Stanton Hill in the mango season!) It was a town to be a boy in.

But Joe's boyhood days were about to be cut short.

Tragedy strikes. Six weeks after their arrival, and nine days before Christmas, Joe's father died. From Joe's account we learn something of customs of the day, and something about the people of the town. By custom, when a funeral passed, shops closed their doors, and men removed their hats. Joe recalled:

My father was buried a pauper. And normally they'd take no notice. But they was that sorry for us that all the business-houses shut their doors – just while we was passing. And it was the custom everybody took their hat off. And they did!

The bewildered gratification of the bereaved family is still palpable in his voice three-quarters of a century later. Buried a pauper but shown respect by all! It was indeed a strange new country they had come to.

There were no Social Service benefits in those days. No Widows Pensions or Child Allowances. Pensions for Civil Widows were not to be introduced until 1942, Child Endowment until 1941. Joe, aged 12, had to become a family bread-winner. We follow him through a range of tough jobs; sweeping the sawdust at Rooney's Sawmill, off-siding to a mean-hearted plumber, doing the sound-effects at the Silent Pictures behind Lowth's Hotel, making 'flong' at the *Bulletin,* washing bottles at the cordial-factory. Anything for a couple of bob. Then, in search of better money, he sets off in unmatched sandshoes after a job on the new railway being built to Alligator Creek meatworks. He gets to be a 'nipper', or water-boy. All day, Joe, undersized for his thirteen years, lugs a four-gallon tin of drinking water up and down the line for the thirsty workmen laying the new track.

Not only do we learn something of the work practices involved but also something of the of the men themselves. A New Chum was a scorned 'Pommy' or a 'Pommy Bastard'. Yet in the traditional mateship of the bush they pitch a tent for young 'Young Pommy Joe', show him how to make a blanket of newspapers in a corn-sack, and a pillow from his boots. They keep a watchful eye on red-headed Kelly O'Halloran, always shaping up for a stoush with the new-comer. You can sense Joe struggling to measure himself against the men he works with and admires, and patterning himself on their example. Very early he takes upon himself the mantle of Aussie Battler, and with it the perceived range of male attitudes; an Aussie will stand by his mates, not be a bludger, regard all bosses with suspicion, women as creatures of another order, gamble, drink and swear. Joe can't get to be one fast enough, (but says he personally never drank nor smoked).

Joe's recall of the shining yesterdays is total. He was fascinated by engines and over half a century later, can describe each that his boyish eyes scrutinized with zestful detail. The engine at the Stanley Picture Show was *a suction gas-producer and a nine-inch cylinder five-foot flywheel, ten-horse-power Carnoff horizontal engine, belt-driven to a hundred and ten volt, sixty-amp generator.*

Joe's story is direct and artless, but in its own way incorporates a range of literary devices. His anecdotes are organized to present a story through a sequence of scenes. His characters, Kelly O'Halloran with 'a face like two mile of bad road'; Mum 'four foot two in her high heels'; McConnel the Plumber 'a bugger of a boss', though mere thumbnail sketches are instantly recognizable. His dialogue is pure theatre. Not only does Joe recall the living words, but in the retelling takes each of the character's parts in turn; The Chinese Herbalist, lisping proudly through gold teeth; Bob Hayles and the bluff McKenzie arguing fares for meatworkers on the launch into town; Artie Olsen advising him to throw in the towel on his first and only boxing-match, are all characters we recognize instantly.

But of chronological sequence there was none. One of Joe's stories could start off in 1913, make a leap forward to the Yanks commandeering civilian cars during the World War Two, table-thump upon how the Mall would turn Flinders Street into a desert, explain where the famous Tree of Knowledge was, digress on to how to cure styes with bread poultices, denounce modern apprentices as not a patch on what they were in his own young days, and finish with a shipboard concert on the 1912 voyage out. All of this at a breathless pace, with many snorts of laughter at his own jokes and remembered tomfoolery.

Oral History interviews should be relaxed and informal times of remembering, and of ordinary conversation not constrained by the structure of formal prose. I have, in transcribing and editing Joe's story, brought the fragments into some semblance of an ordered whole. As Michael Frisch says in A *Shared Authority, Essays on the Craft and Meaning of Oral and Public* History, "why should it be only those in power whose words are selectively edited and presented to the public in polished form? They would have as many 'y' knows', 'Uh.. .'s, hesitations and false starts, if their words were set down exactly as uttered". Joe had little education but had a good mind. I saw it as my role to assemble and even reassemble the bits and pieces of his recollections so that they could be presented as the narrative which he intended.

Joe's swearing was a problem. Though mostly confined to the Great Australian Adjective, it tended to become repetitive. In fact, his swearing was atypical of the other men of the period recorded in the Oral History Collection, most of whom confine themselves to 'My Word!' or, for greater emphasis, 'My Very Word!' I attribute most of Joe's swearing to a larrikin desire on his part to shock the interviewer from the University, in much the same way, as, little lad home from the meatworks for the weekend, he no doubt set about shocking his diminutive mother, to prove his manliness and his new found Aussie Male identity, each 'Christ, Yes!' uttered with an eye to gauging her reaction. I have allowed a few of them in to convey a sense of his character. Joe liked to be thought of as a bit of a hard-case.

Some readers may find Joe's terms for differing ethnic groups offensive. They fall with an ugly clang upon the minds of the more enlightened audience of the late 21st century. However in the post-Federation era of which he is speaking, such words were in common use. For example, 'Chinaman' was as acceptable in everyday English as 'Chinatown' is today, and comparable in usage to 'Indiaman' or 'Macassaman'. Joe does not hesitate to mention himself and his own family as having been seen as "despised Pommies", and himself as a "Pommy Bastard". Such terms are included to convey a sense of the era, and in no way reflect my own personal attitudes.

Disappointingly, Joe never refers, except obliquely, to

World War One. We know from the War Memorial in Anzac Park that, in the years of which Joe reminisces, many a young Townsville man marched away to the Great War never to return. If only Joe had described the recruiting parades, send-offs or patriotic fervour that must have been a feature of those years! It is strange to realize that while the experiences he relates were taking place, other youngsters, brief years older, were landing on the beach at Gallipoli or slogging through the mud of the Somme. Perhaps Joe's struggle for his family's survival in those years was his own personal baptism by fire.

Many of Joe's stories had the well-polished sheen of countless retellings. You could almost feel sympathy for his patient wife, May, offering lemonade or cups of coffee in the background. When inevitably some of Joe's jokes fall flat – who is going to be amused at how some codger in 1915 offered a bar-maid at the Great Northern 'fish and chips' of an old fish-head and chips off the woodheap? – May laughs with practised skill and murmurs 'Yes! You had to make your own fun in those days!' in order to ease the awkward silence. In one or two anecdotes names of characters have been slightly altered to avoid causing possible embarrassment to relatives.

Joe's record of Townsville 1912 to 1918 is of value because such accounts are rare and becoming rarer with the passage of time, and because, given a few inaccuracies here and there – his recall was so detailed. Many of the life histories of the North Queensland Oral History Collection are studded throughout with vague "I wouldn't know about that" or "I don't exactly remember". But Joe has not forgotten. Not only does he remember, but remembers with the clarity of a bright yesterday, and in his zestful retelling invites the listener to slip though a keyhole in time and, for a little while, to wander, with eager-eyed curiosity, the dusty streets of Townsville 1912-1918 with him.

In transcribing Joe Clark's story I grew to appreciate, even to relish, his Ginger Megg cheerfulness, his doggedness, the way he could take a knock and bounce back, his willingness to give things a go, his honesty, his 'guts'. I even liked his incorrigibility. In 1912 Joe had come to Townsville the compleat Immigrant Boy. By the end of his story, 1918, he has, by sheer determination, made himself a dinkum North Queenslander in accent, attitude and spirit. I liked him for it. I hope that readers will too.

SHIPPING NOTES

LIMERICK'S ARRIVAL

The Rippingham Grange, under an alias – the Limerick – arrived in Townsville yesterday from London, with 362 immigrants. Of these there were 33 for Cairns, 44 for Townsville, 50 for Rockhampton and 224 for Brisbane.

The Limerick has also 6500 tons of cargo for Queensland ports, and under her new name has also a new commander, Captain Murdo MacFarlane, who is very popular, well respected, and an expert mariner. His services are highly esteemed in the shipping world.

When the Limerick was known as the Rippingham Grange, she was undoubtedly the most popular vessel in the immigrant passenger business.

The steamer left the Royal Albert docks on July 20th, in glorious weather. From all accounts things have been different since; the shipping troubles in existing in London prevented the steamer sailing on her scheduled date a week earlier. She was fortunate to get away when she did. The weather to Port Said was excellent, there being not a ripple on the water. In fact, to emphasize the calmness, the purser says a rowing boat could have come all the way alone without fear. The heat in the Red Sea, however was terrific, the temperature ranging up to 97 degrees in the shade. The women and children suffered much discomfort in consequence. In the Indian Ocean strong monsoons were experienced, causing the ship to roll very heavily. The usual mal-de-mer was very prevalent. On August 11th very heavy seas struck the Limerick and stove in No 7 lifeboat. From 13th to 20th of that month, heavy rain was experienced. The steamer, however, has made a record voyage, spurred on, no doubt, by her new appellation. She did the trip from London to Thursday Island in 40 days. She averaged over 12 nautical miles an hour.

There has been no sickness among the passengers, worth mentioning, only one case of heat shock occurring. Fainting among the women was, however, common under their new and extreme conditions of heat.

There were frequent entertainments – sports, whist drives, concerts, etc, every week, which went to break the monotony of the six weeks' voyage. On August 14th a most successful children's concert was. given, the youngsters as usual being dubbed with the title of "Morgan's Midgets", after their popular teacher, Purser A Morgan. On the same day the Captain entertained the children at a tea party, which is calculated to live for a long time in their memory. The concerts organised by a musical committee aboard, were all very successful. Messrs Kydd and Blake were most energetic secretaries for the Sports and Entertainment Committee. Mesdames Fisher and Ross were the accompanists. On August 24th a grand farewell concert was held in the afternoon and reflected great credit on those responsible for the entertainment. Six illuminated programes were artistically tinted by Mesdames Clarke and Mackie and they were later drawn for. The raffle resulted in a return of £8/5- which is to be donated to the Brisbane Children's Hospital.

On Monday afternoon, a fancy dress was held and many and varied were the costumes displayed. It was a great succes.

The Purser Mr. Morgan, says he has not received any complaints during the voyage from the passengers.

The passengers are not by any means a wealthy lot, but are endowed with a considerable amount of energy and a desire all round to make fortunes in their new land...

The vessel is expected to leave this afternoon for the South.

The Limerick was formerly the Rippingham Grange and carried troops and horses to the Boer War. She was re-named after being purchased by the New Zealand Steamship Company in 1911 for the immigrant run to the Queensland coast. The Limerick was torpedoed and sunk in 1917 off Bishops Rock.

The Voyage Out – 1912

'And we Come to Townsville'

We left Royal Albert docks in London on the *Limerick*. This was in 1912. I'd have been twelve. I was born at the end of 1899 so I was always the same age as the year. There was my father and mother, my sister and my two brothers. Now, my mother knew Ada Murgatroyd in Charters Towers and she became Mrs. Arrowsmith and they nominated us out. And when you nominated a person you had to keep them so's they wouldn't be on the labour market. The Commonwealth Government paid our fare, ten pounds per family. The shipping company got that. And they had to deliver you. You never got off that ship! They delivered you all right!

The *Limerick* was a three-island job. Poop, stern and centre. She had an old-rust-bucket, three cylinder engine. No immigrants were below decks. We were all above the deck, in the fore-peak; it was half for the men passengers and half for the crew. The men didn't get with the women. They 'wouldn't have none of that there sort of business 'ere' , y' know.

Women and kids were amidships in cabins. We had all of above-decks to ourselves, excepting bar the boat-deck which is where the Old Man, the captain, lived. You never got up there. That was also the quarantine deck, if anything happened. But nothing happened.

We were six weeks coming out and we never got off the ship. We had our rations, which was all worked out. And you only had so much water, but it's enough. You had enough fresh water to wash in. And you had salt-water if you wanted a bath, salt-water by the ton. They even give us the *Townsville Daily Bully* and it was twelve-months old! The purser used to collect papers on his run backwards and forwards. And we would read it, cause you can't get nothin' to read. It was good, generally speaking.

We came through the Bay of Biscay and she give us the bloody lot! And then we got into the Mediterranean, and it's not very rough in the Mediterranean, or it wasn't when we came through. It started to get warmer, and we were Pommies, wrapped up like blankets, y' know. Anyhow, we get to Port Said, and we coaled for eight hundred ton of coal.

They put a barge along side us, and two planks off the barge. And these natives, Gyppos – just dressed in a shirt – and they come up – with those baskets like you kept clothes in – well, it was filled with coal and he caught it on his shoulder, and he run up the plank and he dropped it in the fiddle-hole on the deck and then he chucked the basket down and run down the other plank and somebody else'd load him up again.

And he sung all the time, and the song was 'God give us strength to eat our food so we can work again to eat our food to work again.' This goes on for ever! That was what they told us it was. And they put the Port Said police aboard in case any of these fellows got into the cabins.

Then bum-boats came alongside. A bum-boat is nothing

to do with 'bum'. It's a boat. And it's loaded with fruit. And there's the bum-boat man. And he throws up a rope. And somebody catches it. Then on the end of the rope there's this basket. And then he yells, 'What d'y want?'

And you yell, 'Water-melon!

And he yells back 'Threepence!' And, so, right! You put the threepence in the basket and let the basket down and up comes the water-melon. And the Pommies had never seen a red water-melon. We only seen rock-melons, the yellow ones. So we reckoned they wasn't watermelon. But I ate it. I liked it!

And the bum-boat man throws limes up. There was limes lying on the deck and you got them for nothing. We were supposed to have lime-juice. Lime juice was the regulation, but they didn't spend much money on you. It was supposed to keep blood cool, but it doesn't. But it gives you vitamin C, which you need when you sweat. And so we buy all we can.

And then two fellows get aboard and they sell you a shaddy-wallah, and it was a thing made of clay like a brick. Like an urn. And you fill it with water and it kept cool, like a water-bag, see. Porous clay. And he sells these shaddy-wallahs for about sixpence. And of course when it started to smell you threw it over the side. And then he's selling Turkish fezzes. A flower-pot hat. When it's too big, he bites the corner off and tears it round and keeps tearing it off until –'That'll fit you' – and he fits it on your head.

And we finished coaling, two or three days I think it was – and we're all black as hell, and we head through the Red Sea, and, Gawd, it was hot! And they didn't speed the ship because the stokers just couldn't do it – a coal-fired ship. And they went through the Canal very slowly and the Red Sea very slowly, and they were pulling the stokers out with the ropes. They couldn't get up the stairs. They're pulling them out and laying them in the shade and chucking salty water on them. And they got ice from the refrigeration room. They did their best. We never lost anybody.

And then when we come around from the Red Sea, we didn't stop at Aden, because they said that they'll kill you there. That was what they said. We couldn't get off. And then we come through the Indian Ocean, and we hit the tail end of a cyclone. Well, these ships, the life-boats are hung inside or out. 'Hung in' was on the platform. 'Out' was hanging. Well, if you're going through a storm you hang them out. You don't know if you're going to need'em, see. So all the boats are hanging out. Well, we're coming through this cyclone and a wave come and took two with it. Just like that! And we were four hours standing still. We were all frightened. The engines are tonking away like buggery, but we're just standing still!

There's no radio, no nothing, just depending on people! The ship stood still for four hours, belting this sea. 'That's nothing!' the crew tell the passengers, but they've got the shits too! 'Aw', they tell us, 'That's nothing! You oughta seen us last time!'.

And this bloody sea got me. I'm on the deck, where I shouldn't have been, but I'm a boy, and all boys are curious, else there's something wrong with them. I was on the deck and it washed me down and I hit a bollard, and they pulled me in. Split me nut open! I got a lump on me head that's there still!

A Crossing-the-line ceremony aboard the Limerick *on the immigrant run to Queensland about 1912, with officers and crew-members dressed as King Neptune and his court, to initiate passengers crossing the Equator for the first time. The officer on the right is flourishing a giant 'razor' with which to shave beards. Two curious boys have stationed themselves behind the group. One of them could be Joe Clark.*

But we got out of it. And then there wasn't much more rough weather, only ordinary. We'd lost two boats, but we had the boats what's left, and they looked after them! And we had the concerts. And the Crossing the Line ceremony. That's where the crew dress up to scare hell out of them that hasn't been over the Equator before. Which is all of us! And at the concerts the crew could sing, and so could we. And if you played the fiddle, well you got up and played the fiddle. But I couldn't sing because I had this bloody bandage on my head![1]

Anyway, we were on the same course as people leaving Australia for England. Well, one day – it was a pretty fine day – we had a tub on the mast. And the bloke yelled out that there's smoke in the offing, and we slow down, and so does this other ship, and we were, you might say, three-quarters of a mile apart. They're going that way and we're going this way. He's going that way back to England. But there's no radio. The only news we get is from him. And the only news he can tell England is from us. So they slow down and maybe sometimes stop, and up the first mast goes the house flag, Dalgety's or White Star, and then the ship's name in flags. And then up the other one is different flags, 'Good health' , 'Bad health', 'Death'. You can't read them but they know. The yellow one would be scarlet fever.

And this bloke's got this light – dot and dash. This ship and that ship is doing the same thing, with one man standing and one man reading. Our fellow's saying, 'Good trip. Bin through storm two weeks ago.' And he's going, 'Good health. Plenty of water. Good food. No sickness. And all the bull-shit he's got to say. He's telling us they just come through a storm. We're telling him that we just came through one. And that fellows saying what he's doing, because we'd come to Australia.

And then two blokes gets on the end of the bridge, and

---

1 There must have been other ship-board concerts at which Joe did perform because sixty-eight years later Mrs. M. Croft, of Townsville, who had not seen Joe in the intervening years, could still remember his singing. She was a three year old passenger on the 'Limerick' on the same voyage, and recalls thinking how grown-up Joe seemed because he was wearing long trousers.

they're doing the Boy Scouts' flags, semaphore. And they're making like buggery at the same time. And we give 'em our news. And then they decide they're gettin' too far away. And both ships get up steam slowly.

Because when he gets back to England; 'Seen the *Limerick?*' 'Oh! We passed her such-and-such a date! No sickness.' And that's what they want to know. And did we get here! When we got here the cable would tell them but nobody knew until they got a cable from Australia.

Well, anyhow, we get towards Torres Strait. Now, these captains, if they could get across the sandy shoal, which is shallow, it would save them – say they gotta go right round the shoal, it would take a day. They go across the shoal if the tide was right. And they would save that much steam. The captain wanted to get over this shoal because he'd save a day's steaming going round the other way, the Torres Strait.

So they had the bosun – and he had a platform sticking out the side of the fore-well, on the right hand side, which is the starboard. And he had a lead, the shape of a Saxa Salt, a lump of lead with a hole in the bottom. And he had a piece of white rope, and every six feet of that rope was a piece of flag-bunting, red, green and all that. Well, that was a fathom, six feet.

Well, then he'd stand on this platform and the ship slowed down, until it's just moving. And the bosun would take this thing, and he's in this platform, above deck height, on the hand-rail, and he'd swing it see. He'd keep swinging it for a long while, and then he give it a good swing, right ahead. He'd let it go, and it would drop into the ocean.

And then he'd grab it, and when it comes perpendicular, he pulls it up as fast as he can, and watches where the bunting is. Then he yells out, 'By the mark! Six!' Which means six fathoms. Then, 'By the mark! Four!' Four fathoms. And the mate was there too, watching the mark. There was no mistakin'! 'By the mark! Six!' And the mate was writing it down.

And the old carpenter, 'Chippie' they called him, he says, 'The bloody Old Man's groping his bloody way to Australia again!' Anyhow, we pick up the Torres Strait pilot, and he brings us to Thursday Island. And we drop him over. We can't get off. We're not allowed off! And then we come down to Cairns. And the Cairns mob get off and all their mattresses get burnt. They won't have English wogs in Australia! But there's no wogs, because the ship is steam-cleaned and it's cleaned with sulphur. They burned sulphur in a ship. And it'll kill any cockroaches. Nothing will live in sulphur-dioxide gas. A sulphur candle, they call it. They seal the ship and burn sulphur. They got to do it. You can smell it when you get on board a ship. And this smart bloody wharf-lumper fetches cascara-beans on board and gives 'em us, and everybody gets the shits.

And we come to Townsville and we get off. There was no pass-port. My old man had some sort of a receipt, but that was all. It was still part of England. And of course, we were Pommies. And some say it was got from 'pomegranate' to 'immigrant'. And we were no good. Australians wouldn't accept you because you were a Pommy. And they're Pommy descendants themselves! But when you worked alongside 'em and you wasn't a bludger then they'd say, 'Oh, he's all right! He's not a bad poor bugger'. Like a man accepts a man. But not until you're proven. You're not going to put nothing over the Australian! He's not going to let you. So if you're working with them, you do your share! Oh, well, we kept our end up!

And of course, when we came here, I loved the country, because it's so free and easy. My mother liked it until my old man died – he died a few weeks after we got here. She wanted to go back. She asked her mother for money to go back and her mother wouldn't cough it up. And, by gee, she never wrote to her mother again. Never forgave her. But it's a funny thing! One day we were sitting on the verandah, and she says, 'My mother just died!' And I told her, 'Oh, bullshit!' And she said, 'She just died!'

Anyhow, a few weeks later we get a letter and her mother had died. And Mother had got it to the minute! But it was a good job she didn't give her the money, anyhow! She wanted to go back. But I wouldn't have been a bloody Australian if she did!

Castle Hill from the Pilot Station, as it might have appeared to the Clark family on arrival in 1912

The Newcomers – 1912

When we first come we lived where the road goes through Stanley Street up the Cutting. Well, that Cutting wasn't built then. We lived on the right hand side opposite the Sacred Heart. On the hill.

The butcher with a cart served everybody on the road, but we were off the road, so the hill-butcher used to take us. He had a horse, with one long stirrup and one short one. The meat basket sat on the short stirrup on his knee and on the saddle. And when he come to the house, he'd take the meat out of the basket and slam it on the picket-fence. He'd sing out, 'Butcher!' and, bang, on the picket it went. And of course, you got down before the big bull-ants got it! Because they'll get it fast!

Anyhow, my Old Man, being a Pommy, thought this was crude. He was shocked. And he couldn't hammer a nail, but he gets hold of a packing-case and he nails it on the rail of the fence, and he puts this china-plate on it. And the next morning, the butcher comes. 'Butcher!' And he bangs the meat down. Breaks the plate, and there goes the meat! Gawd! My Old Man never got over that!

And the butcher, whatever meat you wanted tomorrow, say, 'Two pounds of rump steak', you wrote it on a piece of paper, and you got that same piece of paper stuck on. You couldn't get it off. He stuck it on when it was warm and sticky, and when you went to cook it your own writing was still on it. Beef was only about tuppence; corned-beef was about tuppence ha'penny the pound. You always had corned-beef because it kept. The offal was cheap. Oxtail nearly for nothing. Liver, well, nobody wanted liver, only the dog. And you could buy sweetbread; and you'd get a whole bullock's kidney for about threepence.

The milk when it come in the morning was hot milk from the dairy. He came in and filled our billy-can. And you had to boil it. We had a round crockery gadget like a flat disk with spiral-grooves on the underneath and about a quarter-inch hole in the middle. And you put that in the bottom of the saucepan to stop it burning.

Our house had no lino, just scrubbed pine floors. There was no inside plumbing, just a tap at the back steps. The town water came from Aplin's Weir and was no good.[2] We had a rag tied on the tap and when it got full of mud we chucked that away and put another piece on. Everybody had tanks. And the water-bag was part of your house. We'd have a water-bag hanging down below. It was cool but it got slimy inside. If you boiled 'em you ruined 'em. Boiling canvas ruins it. So you'd try to get the slime out by putting sand in it and shaking it up and down. The best water-bag was a sheet of canvas and you tied it up by the four corners. And then you could turn it inside out and do the same to the other side.

And there was Willy-John Foley, used to come up with the baker's cart. And he couldn't get up the hill so he walked up with his basket of bread, no paper on the bread, his sweat and all on it, but that doesn't matter! Threepence a loaf, a two pound loaf. The baker's cart was like a box on wheels, and he rode on the top of the box. The door was at the back. And Willy-John would stop the horse, get off, open the back door, take the bread out, and he'd walk with his basket and deliver the bread. And then when he came back he'd chuck the basket in the wagon and slam the door. And when he slammed the door the horse would start to walk off to the next customer. Which he knew! Well, as soon as he's gone off, us kids'd slam the door,

---

2 Joe's memory is a little off-track on this one. Aplin's Weir was built in 1928. Prior to that, town water was supplied from two wells, Willmett's, opposite Mundingburra School, and Hubert Well at Aitkenvale. A stop-weir of steel sheeting driven through the sand to the clay bed was built in 1927; the permanent concrete weir in 1943, during the water-shortages occasioned by the wartime presence of up to 90,000 servicemen. The water may well have been of dubious quality necessitating the 'rag on the tap' in the Dry Season.

and the horse would walk off up the road and here's Willy-John up the hill! Oh, he used to go crook!

And the grocer, he came and delivered all your stuff in a case, a timber case – there was no card-board cases then. And then you gave him next week's order, and when he came next week, he puts it all out in front of you, jam, butter, pickles, and so on, and you pay him for last week's stuff, and give him next week's order. And you make him a cup of tea.

And to clean our teeth we used salt. But many people used that cuttle-fish you get on the beach for cocky's cages. And there was Chinese tooth-paste. It come in little wooden boxes. Us kids used to reckon it was made of Chinamen's bones ground up.

Always a success with *Dr. Waugh's* unequalled *Baking Powder*

Young Housekeepers (and the more experienced also) as well as the boys and girls, suffer grim disappointment if anything goes wrong with the cake in the baking. Those who are wise will be sure to obtain and use "Dr. Waugh's Baking Powder" – only "Dr. Waugh's" – which is unequalled for all purposes, and makes everything deliciously light and wholesome. Try the new tin with patent lever lid.

At home we had table-lamps, kerosene, and the front room had a hanging chandelier-type lamp, which was very bright and consumed a bottle of kero a night, so it didn't get used very often. We bought kerosene from the grocer at eight bob a case, two four gallon tins, all Vacuum, American. And we had a kerosene-pump to get it out, which was a tin affair with a marble for a trip valve.

We kept the butter cool in a stump-cap on the back table. The stump-cap was filled with water to keep the ants out, and the butter was left under an ordinary flower-pot with a rag cover, and it kept as cool as you would want it.

The Coolgardie safe was made of hessian. It was a safe made of zinc iron and framed with a trough on the top. And the hessian came up the side and dropped into the trough. And the trough was kept full of water and the water by capillary action would get down to the bottom trough and evaporate. So it was always wet and cool. It could keep your meat cool. And your milk.

We had a wood-stove, a Beacon Light. We bought wood-blocks for twelve and six a load, about half a ton. The blocks were never straight-grained, and my brother and me had to chop enough wood on Sundays to last all the week. My mother was a past master at the stove and corned beef, cooked with vinegar, cloves, molasses, and peppercorns, was out of this world.

Our great favourite was Meat Billy Pudding. She'd get an Ironbark pumpkin and cut out a large plug out of the top and scrape out all the seeds and fill it up with chopped-up beef – shin-beef, small dumplings and a rasher of bacon, and the condiments, and then put the plug back with the pastry and boil it in the cloth. There'd be enough for the whole family. Another one was, get a large paw-paw and scoop the seeds out and fill it with blancmange and jelly.

Saturday arvo we had to clean the knives on the board with knife powder, which was emery dust, then polish the spoons and forks, fill up the lamps and polish the glass, and trim the wicks. And clean out the fowl-house and rake up the yard, and repair your boots, and clean the outside of the windows. Any time I had a stupid idea of belting a ball around, my good-hearted mother would tell me that there was a poor old lady up the street and she needs her wood chopping. She'd say, 'Our Joey would be only too pleased to do it'. But on Sunday arvos we'd go down to the jetty-wharf and be shown over a ship, and see the engines.

They didn't know that mossies brought anything then. Though malaria was here when I was a boy. And when you got the flu, it was a pneumonic thing on your chest. And the cure was Antiflogestine. And it came in a tin and you boiled your tin. It was like putty. And you got a knife and you slapped it on a lump of rag – red hot – and you put it on his chest. And you bandage him up. Then the linseed poultice. And they used to give it to the fowls afterwards 'cause the fowls would eat linseed.

My father died. He was a tailor and he had a job to go to direct we got here but we'd only been here no more'n four, five weeks and he died. And he was buried a pauper, and normally people'd take no notice. But they was that sorry for us being New Chums and mother with four of us, that all the business-houses shut their doors – just while we were passing. And it was the custom everybody took their hat off. And they did! If you were driving a buggy and a funeral was passing, you stop the buggy and you take your hat off just to show respect for that man. They did that for my father. And he was buried in the New Cemetery about twelve rows back.

Joseph Clark who died shortly after the family's arrival in 1912

So then we were broke. We had no money, and we've got to live, so I get a job sweepin' the floor at Rooney's Saw-mill. I'd be twelve. Rooney's Mill was where Rooney's Bridge is now. There was no road to Rooney's and in the wet weather I'm up at seven and we walked along the railway line to get to work. It was a big saw-mill which employed, oh, perhaps a hundred men. Steam driven, and we were cutting logs five foot in diameter, silky oak logs, and they came up Ross River in the sailing-ships. They came from the Tablelands, by sailing-ship from Cairns. They came up the river, which is non-existent now – its flattened out, because the Charters Towers mob burnt all the mangroves. The *Shark* and the *Swordfish* were the boats, and also the *Seoul*.

So I'd sweep the floor and Bill Browning'd come along with the wheelbarrow and took the sawdust away. Oil the machines on the floor. And you have your dinner there, and then you worked in the afternoon till five o'clock, and walked home. I got seven bob a week.

And I'm working at the Stanley Pictures at night, getting one-and-six for making the sound-effects and two bob for selling the lollies. I'd have to be down there at seven to start the motor, and out the back till eleven, so it was midnight when I got home. And I'm up at seven. See! I'd fall asleep in the mill. I've got caught many a time. You'd get your arse kicked. I've had my backside kicked a thousand times! It was a punishment to get a kick. If you gave him cheek, he'd wheel you round and give you the boot! That was customary. If you were smart you never got the boot. You were faster than him. But I was never fast enough!

Then there was the 'flu epidemic. We were scared! People were dying! They were dying like rats. They didn't know where it come from. And the doctors told you: Anything a fly can get on, burn it![3]

And my mother used to give us ammoniated tincture of quinine. God it was horrible stuff! It was even parts of ammonia – refrigeration ammonia – and quinine. Mixed

---

3 Perhaps Joe is confused about the date of the 'flu epidemic. Immediately after the Great War of 1914 - 1918 an epidemic of pneumonic influenza, commonly known as the Spanish flu swept the world. In Townsville public meetings were banned and picture theatres and schools closed. About one in four people contracted the disease. There were eighteen deaths. There may have been previous bouts of seasonal influenza which Joe is confusing with this.

together. It's the most nauseating thing you can take. Only a few drops in sugar. And another one was sulphur and treacle. But we always had to take it. It was supposed to clean your blood. She'd buy a packet of sulphur and then you got, say, half a cup of treacle, and about as much sulphur as would fit on a penny, and you mix the two together. And it wasn't a bad taste. We used to eat it. I don't know what it did for you but when it comes out it makes you shit yellow. And another one was senna tea. It's nauseating sweet. You can get it down but it stops in your throat. You got to eat dry bread after it.

And she'd make all sorts of things up. She made some charcoal tablets – which was burnt charcoal, and gum-Arabic and sugar and peppermint flavour, and she rolls it out on a board and then she cuts it into lollies that are about an inch and a half big, and then you all had to have charcoal tablets which was good for the stomach. And I had the dengue fever – we called it 'the dingo' – and Mum says, 'That's the stomach!' So down goes four charcoal tablets.

So I goes to walk to work; I had no push-bike or nothing. I'm only a kid! Railway Estate wasn't built then. There was nothin' on it. Not till about 1916 when the gold in Charters Towers started to give out, and most folks come to Townsville and found jobs. There was a bloke by the name of Stan Nolan owned most of Railway Estate and he was selling off blocks at twenty-five quid a quarter-acre. And people brought their houses down from Charters Towers but they had to cut them down to eight feet to get them in the railway trucks. Colonial homes had ten foot walls, well they had to saw two foot off the top to get them in the trucks! That's how Railway Estate got started. Before that there was nothing. No roads. We walked along the railway line, one track.

And, this day, I get to Rooney's Mill and I'm sick. And Fred Rooney come along, and he says, 'Come on. I'll take you home.' So he puts me in the buggy and takes me home. And they were building that Cutting road at that time and a chap named Dan Galvin was the stone-fixer – that's the man who fixes the stone for the wall. And when Fred fetched me home I'm real sick, and we lived opposite the Sacred Heart church. I jumped out of the buggy and I'm gonna spew, and I ran over to this stone-fixed wall and I spewed on the wall and it was black.

And Mrs. Miller, further up round Hale Street, was coming home in a hansom-cab. It's a real hot day, and I'm spewing black against this wall. Well, she went back and she said, 'That kid down there, he's spewing as black as a crow!'

Well, it wasn't long that the word got round that the Clarks was eatin' crows! And of course, we didn't know. I was sick. And Old Miller come down, and he says, 'How are you, Joe?'

And I says, 'Oh, not bad.'

And he goes over to Dan Galvin as is putting the stone up, and he says, 'How you doing, Dan?'

And he says, 'Oh, All right. Yeah.' And he says, 'Pommy Joe's crook!'

And he says, 'Yeah! You know,' he said , 'I heard that they're eatin' bloody crows, the poor buggers.'

And he says, Yeah! And you know I can't get within shootin' distance of them bastards!'[4]

But people were good. They helped. After my father died, the men at Rooney's used to stand me up and make me sing and then pass the hat round. They did a lot of nice things. And somebody would give me an orange out of his crib. And somebody'd give me a boiled egg. Whatever they could give you, they'd give, with a cheerful heart! And Mum'd order a three-pound roast for us, because that's all we could afford, and

---

4 Anyone who has ever tried to shoot a crow will appreciate the humour of this anecdote. Crows will ignore the presence of humans until anything even resembling a rifle is pointed in their direction, whereupon they decamp with bullet-defying celerity.

she'd get a five! And you'd pay your butcher's bill, you'd pay him once a week, and he'd give you a lump of German sausage. Around midday on a Saturday the butcher would practically be giving meat away. No refrigeration so they couldn't keep it. So the soup-pot and the crab-pot were well looked after. And you'd pay your baker and he'd give you a dozen buns. And you paid your grocer and he'd give you a packet of lollies. People were good.

There was always some neighbour killing a goat. Everybody had goats. There were thousands of them! In the main street and all. There was no weeds. They ate the bloody lot! Some of them was Saenen goats, Swiss goats, which had the two bells on them. But the milk was just the same. When a goat had three or four kiddies, people'd kill a kiddie, and kiddies are lovely meat. It's mutton. So if he killed a goat next door, he can't eat it all and there's no refrigeration so he sends it over. You'd get a leg and the chops and whatever you want. People shared.

The creek was full of fish and crabs. The breakwater's full of oysters; it was just a matter of going out and helping yourself. There was no way of keeping anything so you just took what you could eat. Rowes Bay's full of prawns! The Common's full of ducks! And if you went fishing and you got more than you could eat, well, you had no refrigeration, you give it away. When a man went duck-shooting, he'd give you four or five ducks. That's how we lived. And it was a good way.

We went to bed with the chooks and got up at cockcrow. There was one tap by the back steps and another in the outside bathhouse. We washed our feet more often than our faces what with all the horses and goats and chooks and dogs. We had no boots. The drain was channelled off to the fruit trees, and the washing-day also helped. We had every fruit! Custard-apples, paw-paws! Mangoes you'd bump your head on going along the road! Every yard had a lemon tree in, and women used the lemon – believed in lemon something like The Pill.

We all used to eat tamarinds. A tamarind, well, it looks like a turd, it's brown and it falls off the tree, and it's got a crackly skin on it. You can break it off, like a light shell. And inside it's got three knobs in, like three seeds. And between the seeds is the lemoniest thing going – you can file your teeth off with it!

And you can shake 'em in a bottle with a bit of sugar, and make a tamarind drink.

The cascara bean, it's a long thing like a sausage, and it's a hard shell, and you can break it open, and every shell is a seed with this licorice flavoured goo on it. And you take the shells out and you lick them And then you throw that part away and break some more out. I used to love it! But it will put you out of circulation for the day! Oh! Fast! And good!

And Chinee apples! They're a dry-bitter. They make your tongue bloody-awful, a Chinee apple does. And you want a pair of gloves to pick them because they're that bloody prickly! And then you've got guavas, which was always loaded with maggots. You don't see it until you've broke it open when you've half eaten them! Nothin' worse than a half a maggot.

Everybody grew bananas to mop up the waste-water from washing-day and the bath-house, and if you had banana-trees, you'd cut the bunch, and you'd take a hand over to your neighbour. Because nobody can eat a bunch of bananas! If you eat six that's all you eat before the rest went rotten, so you'd give 'em away. And that's how we lived in the early days. And we had the granadillas. And if you wanted passion-fruit you went to the cemetery and got them. Passion-fruit and gherkins, wild gherkins! Growing wild down the cemetery. You go out there and they're hanging from grave to grave.

Where Reid Park is now, that was Monkey Island, on the side of Ross Creek. You could go across in a boat or at low tide you could walk across, it was up to your waist. The Chinamen there grew pineapples, watered by salt-water, stunted things, but sweet! Twelve a shilling They reclaimed that and now it's where the theatre is.

Houses were seldom locked up because there was nothing to steal inside. The hanging-safe and the water-bag were on the outside! People were mostly poor but we probably lived better than most people today. Everyone shared. And there was so much to be got free.

Flinders Street East, about 1913.

Flinders Street – 1913

'She Was a Good Town!'

Now, down the bottom end of Flinders Street was a wharf and a shed for cargo, which was generally Adelaide Shipping Company. And that was at what they call the Swing Basin. No big ships came up here but the *Mourilyan* and *Kuranda* and the lighters. To turn round they had to turn in the Swing Basin to head out to sea. That's how it got the name. The big wharf was still being built out to sea.

And alongside the shed was big yards where the horses and wagons used to go to unload to get the stuff on to that wharf. And that road is half as wide again as Flinders Street because they had to turn the bullock teams. You can't back bullocks. You lead bullocks. You got the wagon and you lead them up and you hook'em up. They won't back. So that street was big enough to turn the bullock-teams to come out again.

When you come up past the Customs House on the corner of King Street, on the other corner was the Imperial Hotel. In them days, the boarders dragged their beds on the verandah because it was too hot in the room. So if you was going down the road you'd probably hear the housemaid singing while she was making the beds. That's the only noise you'd hear! And the men in the bar.

And next was Wilcox and Moffat's store. That stunk to high heaven. That was the hides. Flies and hides! And on the other side was still more yards, and sheds full of wool. And past Ramages's Hotel there was a Chinese shop and then there was BPs.[5] BPs was a big three-storey place. Us kids used to reckon the top storey was all mouth-organs and glass beads for trade-goods for the Kanakas. We never seen a Kanaka. But BP's had a name for black-birding, and we reckoned 'That's full of mouth-organs up there!' But it was a crockery store up there.

Then there was a long series of sheds – shops they were – and in one, strangely enough, was an aeroplane that landed on Ross River. A stick and string affair. And they'd charge threepence to see it. It was an aeroplane that somebody had dropped on Ross River! I never knew who did it.[6] They pulled them shops down and made it one long store, and on a big tide there'd be water in that store.

Up the street was the Bank of New South Wales, which was on the other corner. Behind that was a boarding-house. Used to be the first post-office, but it was a boarding-house in my young days. And then, next door to the bank was P.F. Hanran's store, which was a grocery store. And then next to that was an ice-works run by Buchanans. We used to say we could smell the 'harmonia' in the street!

---

5 James Burns began business in Townsville in 1873 as a storekeeper and shipping agent, with Robert Philp. By 1883 business interests in Sydney and Queensland had been amalgamated under the name Burns, Philp & Co , and included ventures in storekeeping, timber-getting and the pastoral industry which helped pioneer the development of areas of North Queensland and the Pacific.

6 The first aeroplane in Townsville landed at Cluden racecourse in 1913. Special trains were laid on to enable people to see it, and some joy-rides were given. Possibly this is the same plane.

And then there was Lang's Hotel, the Commercial, but they called it the Blood Hole, because of all the fights. And then Wilmett's Store. They had everything. Everything! Because that block was populated then. That was the main end of town, the busy end. The population was near the creek and the hill, but nothing much away anywhere else.

There were more pubs then that what we got now. Miles more. Ten thousand people. They must have drank a hell of a lot! Sixpence a pint! Knock'em over like buggery! They weren't spirit-drinkers. They'd call spirits Lunatic Soup! And they weren't wine drinkers. They were beer-drinkers. And the beer came up in casks from Melbourne. There was no brewery here. There was one, called the Lion Brewery, and then someone put this thing on the cemetery fence, 'Drink Lion Beer and you'll be lyin' here!' It wasn't any good because the water wasn't any good.[7]

Right opposite Hayles', that was a bank. They've turned it into a rooming house now. You seen the big columns? Beautiful!

---

7 This joke was circulating as early as 1902. Joe was not one to let the chance of a good joke slip and obviously cannot resist adding it in.

And Old Jack Hayles, he had a Captain Kettle beard![8] And he had this boat called the *Magnet* and it had a Petta kerosene engine. Used to go Boingk! Boingk! Boingk! Wasn't very powerful but it got him out of the creek. And when he got out he'd stop the engine, and if you was going to the island, he'd sail it. And you get to the island eventually maybe. But you sailed. And if he lost the wind, he'd start the engine; Boingk! Boingk! Boingk! And he had four boys, Bob, Jack, Charlie, and ... Ben.

And then there was a lot o' small shops until you got to Rooney's – which sold you rifles, and cement, and hardware. And three-ply, which was a novelty. Wasn't much good, but.

Then further up there was Chinamen's shops. We used to go to the Chinaman's to have a drink. He'd sell you soft-drink off the ice. If you give him threepence, he'd give you a bottle and two glasses. We used to go in for a drink. He'd sell you lollies. He'd sell you fruit and vegetables. They stocked everything that a small shop would stock, and all the sort of junk that you would expect off a Chinaman because it came in pretty cheap in them days. Chinese fans, Chinese slippers, those bamboo curtains. A lot of stuff came in over the coast that we didn't know about.

All these old Chinamen in the gardens. They came in on a ship and were dumped up the coast and nobody knew anything about it. And another old Chinaman would see him and say, 'Oh! He my brother!' And they'd take them and work them for nothing! And the old fellows they took to opium because it was the only thing in their life.

---

8   Robert Hayles (Snr) built a two-storey hotel at Picnic Bay on Magnetic Island in 1899 on the site of the original Quarantine Reserve. He built a jetty and had a steam-ferry in operation, possibly the forerunner to the 'Magnet'.

The Imperial Hotel where housemaids could be heard singing in the morning as they make the beds on the verandahs. Beyond the hotel is the row of shops inside one of which Joe Clark remembers a 'stick and string' aeroplane being display for threepence a look in 1913.

The Chinese, us kids called them Chinks or Pongs. Or Chows. The older ones used to bring all their hair back and they'd make a bun. But if they had a pig-tail we used to give it a jig now and then! But most of them used to roll it up and put it inside this little round, black cap. In the street they'd put it in there in case you pulled their pig-tail, you see! We used to wait just to torment them.

One old chap, had long hair, down to his waist, plaited. Black! Too black for him. And greasy. They used to oil them. And I give it a tug, and the bloody hat come off! It was just a bloody wig! And he was chasing me, yelling, 'Lallikin!' (he means 'Larrikin') 'Stop him! Trip him!' And I'm galloping! And I got out the way! He was good on the toe but I was better!

The old Chinamen that appealed to the people were the ones that had their own horse and cart and used to come round with the vegetables and fruit. You didn't have to go shopping for that. He come three times a week.

We had a Chinese doctor, too, Quong Su Duck. He was a herbalist. He had the gold teeth and the blue umbrella. Chinamen always had the blue umbrella, real cheap, made in China. And he used to come along with his little dilly-bag of aniseed, or whatever, and he'd, 'Eh! heh! Heh!' And his gold teeth'd nearly fall out. He had a mouth full of gold teeth. Gold teeth were very common.

But the Chinese doctors was good! They had good cures! Now Mum had a crook eye once, styes. They were really like pimples, the styes. And Leong Louie come along, and he said, 'I fix it!' And he had something in a raspberry leaf, honey and something, and he said, 'You put this on', and it fixed the eye! They had their good cures.

Quong Su Duck had all these things.

And there was a Jap shop which sold Japanese fans and mats, and curtains; kiminos, with paintings on the back. All that sort of thing. And silks, nothing but brilliance, blacks and reds. And there was a bank on the corner of Denham Street which is the Perc Tucker Gallery now, and you go across the road and there was the Tree of Knowledge. Between Hayles and that corner there was nothing. There was no shops. There was a Ladies' Rowing Club there.

Next door to the Post Office was the Trades Hall. On the top was the Union, and underneath was Poultney's, and Stanley Moore the Dentist. And old Mrs 'Whosit', Mrs Mendham, was on the top. When she answered the phone she'd say, 'Who's it?' So they called her 'Mrs. Whosit'!

And next door was the Fire Brigade.[9] And the Fire Brigade was built on a rubbish-heap and the floor was like that! (sloping) And they put the engine on and it collapsed. There was a tower with N.S.E.W. on it. That tower was for drying hoses. See, they pull the hoses up and dry them after a fire, and for the men to practise jumping out of three or four storeys.

There was a bell there. And when there was a fire they'd give the bell a hell of a pull. You could hear it all over town. There wasn't any other noise, see. You'd always stop when you heard the fire-bell, and say, 'Listen! Listen!' And if it was One, Two, Three. That was for West End! And we all take off for West End! And then we'd wreck some poor bugger's house getting his stuff out, thinking we're helping the Fire Brigade!

At first they had horses but then they got a Denys Fire Engine which came from England on the boat. And Harry Lewis, he was a voluntary fireman, he's gonna start a carrying business. And he buys the fire-brigade horse, lively thing it was, corn-fed. And next time the fire-bell goes off, the engine takes off, and the horse is galloping after it! It was that used to the excitement and the bell! And Harry, he can't hold him, and

9 Established 1886, the Fire Station remained on this site until 1926 when it was moved to Walker Street. In 1977 it was moved to the present site in South Townsville.

he's fallen down and he's bouncing around in the bottom of his own cart! He can't even stand up! And the horse is chasing the bloody fire-brigade!

And next to the Council Buildings was the Theatre Royal. I sang in that in 1913 when Harry Clay came up. He had a waxworks and vaudeville show. And he had a singing competition and I won. If Vic Foley knew I was going to sing no matter what he played I could do it. I had a job as a stage-hand, Spare Man, and if anything goes wrong on the stage well, the Spare Man jumps in. I'd have been thirteen, fourteen.

And they didn't have zippers in them days, only hooks and eyes. And once this girl was going to go on and I seen that all the hooks at the back of her dress were come undone and there's nothing holding the back. And I said, 'Get Back!' And I jump on to the stage and I'm walking up and down talking to the audience, pulling their legs, and then Vic Foley gets the music up off the floor and he starts up, and I start and I do my stuff. And then this kid gets her dress fixed up and she's ready to go on again. That's a Spare Man. I did it all the time at the Theatre Royal. You get no money for it but you have a lot of fun.

In 1913 Townsville hadn't got electric power laid on. There was a few electric plants in town, at the Queensland Hotel, which had a billiard table, and the Geisha Cafe and the Picture Shows and McGinnis's Billiards Rooms of five tables and card rooms, the barber's shop with four chairs and a bookmaking shop in the front. They were all suction-gas jobs, fuelled with charcoal. The voltage of all of these was 110 volts, about forty-candle power. The rest of the places were illuminated by carbide generators. And town-gas,[10] and petrol light. The carbide was a small gasometer, made of two galvanized-iron tanks, one inside the other, and fed with lump carbide, which came in drums, from H. L. Jones and Co. of Tasmania, and cost sixpence a pound.

The streets had gas-lights with mantles. The gas-works was situated at the bottom of Stanley Street, on the bank of the creek. The gas-works had a wharf at the back and coal came from Newcastle by ship, which was lightered up the creek on

---

10   Townsville's streets had been lit by gas-lamps since 1904. They were extinguished at midnight and when the moon was full, not lit at all.

a steam-lighter, named the *Bobby Towns*. The gas was laid on in the hotels by one-eighth diameter copper tubes. Some of them had petrol-lights which was a pressure cylinder, two foot six high, complete with a filler cap and a pressure gauge and fastened on the side was a manual pressure pump for air. The lamps had mantles.

And past the Alexander Hotel there was Carrols. Carrols was a boot store in them days. Rushes owned it. They had one of those wires that went up to the office on the top floor with the dockets in it. Then there was McKimmins on the corner, McKimmin and Richardsons, it was then. And Bert Brown's the Tobacconist, and Armati's Chemist shop and Clayton's.

Clayton's was a very old-time chemist and he had a thing like a chest of drawers, all little drawers, and in them was all the things that you would use to make a remedy. And he boiled these flowers and things and got the essence of them. And he had pink string and sealing wax. And everything he wrapped up in paper and did it nice, and then tied it with pink string. And he had a little gas-flame going all the time and he put the sealing-wax in the flame and dabbed sealing wax on the knot. And when you got pills, the pill-boxes weren't like bottles, they were made of shaving. Somebody had planed a shaving off a board and it was bent round and clipped. The lid was a shaving, too, with staples. And if you wanted an ointment, it was still in the wooden box. The grease'd come through.

Where T.R.E.B. was later was the Lyceum Pictures. The Court House Hotel was across the road. And the hansom-cabs and cars was on the middle of the street. And then you had an empty paddock with just a bit of a shack on and you could buy penny lollies there. And there was Horn and Peterson's and the Grand Hotel. And Inglis Smith's. There were plenty of drapers. People didn't buy one yard of flannelette, they bought twelve. If you was making pyjamas for the boys you had to make for them all! And flannel shirts, Jackie Howes. You got it cheaper buying by the bolt.

HOW DO YOU

JUDGE A FLANNELETTE?

By the appearance, the feel—and the price? . Very good. But, unfortunately, few women are sufficiently acquainted with the technical details of cotton manufacture to rely on their own judgment alone. This emphasises the necessity of buying according to standards THAT ARE KNOWN TO BE ACCURATE, backed by a trade mark that guarantees quality and insures the best that can be woven. This unfailing guide is the stamp of **OSMAN**, which appears on the selvedge of the best Flannelette.

And past the New Zealand Insurance Company was the tailoring shop, Hillman's, where my old man worked when we first come. And there was Hulbert's O.K. Store. And Holiman's toy shop. And Lowth's Hotel was on the corner and they had the Stanley Picture Show, which was open-air with a corrugated-iron fence around it. I worked there at night after my old man died. I was the Sound Effects Boy. I got one and six a week and two-bob to take the lollies and chocolates around.

There were horse buses and they would stop anywhere for you. Middle of the block or anywhere. Didn't make any difference. Just pull the bell. Horse buses had two seats across the front and then the big long cab at the back. The men never got in there. They'd sit at the front and dangle their legs over the shafts, see. The bus would be about half as long as a standard bus now, and it was pulled by two horses. But if it was hot weather he had four horses. The horses got a fair crack. And he'd do two trips to town a day. And in the wet weather it was four horses. He'd pull up and stop anywhere for you. You only paid when you got off. Threepence. You didn't pay when you got on.

And old Charlie Beale was a crabby old bugger. And one time this old dame gets in, and she's in the back with the basket, see. She's got a live fowl, and she's taking it to her daughter's, to kill for tomorrow. And he starts off, and he looks back and he says, 'Hey! Missus! You can't have bloody livestock on the bus.' And he says, 'You can't do that! A bloody live fowl! Gawd-Orl-Bloody-Mighty! They'll shoot me!' And he's going on. And she pulls the bell. And he stops the bus, and she gets off and wrings the chook's bloody neck, and gets back on. And she's saying,

'How about that! Bloody Charlie Beale! How about that!' And he said, 'Bloody women!' and he hits the horse!

And us kids'd get on the back and have a free ride, you know. And Charlie could put that whip right round our backsides. And then Billy Rose married one of his daughters and Billy was a motor-mechanic and Billy rigged a Ford Spark-coil, and he puts it across the two hand-rails of the back stairs to give the kids a shock and knock 'em off. When the kids are hanging on the back you press the button and they fall off! And one day Charlie Beale's having a beer at Lowth's, and he says 'There's the bloody bus!' and he runs out and he goes to get on at the back. And Billy hits the button and arse-over-tip goes Charlie! Gawd! Talk about laugh!

And down in Flinders Lane – that's Ogden Street now, there were a lot of old places where the girls were on the game, single-verandah houses from the early days and they'd rent them. Behind Pages. There'd be seven or eight in that block. They did a good trade as there were plenty of men about, meatworkers and locals. But there were no rape cases and not much crime. Us kids used to go down and look at 'em! And up near the *Bulletin,* there was another five that way. There was never any trouble. All the sailing-ships came here. And the crew came in and they did all right. They'd generally hit the first brothel, the first pub, the first gaol, then back on the ship. Also in Flinders Lane was Vardy's Iceworks driven by a Hornsby suction-gas engine. The ice was threepence a block and run like hell before it melts.

There were other ways we could earn a few pennies;

washing bottles in the cordial factory, sweeping the shop footpaths before eight o'clock when they opened. The shop-keepers didn't want all the horse-muck off the street coming in on their floors. Or you could be holding someone's horse for them while they were in the pub or doing their shopping. You'd maybe get threepence. Or running messages for people. I used to do a paper-run too, selling the *Bulletin*. You'd pay a penny each for them and sell them for a penny ha'penny. All in a cut down chaff-bag.

Flinders Street wasn't made. It was all dirt. You could drop a hat in a hole in Flinders Street and never see it. In the Wet of course the cabs just walloped into it. If the womenfolk were just going to take off to cross over they'd get it all on their skirts.

She was a good town!

Central Flinders Street, 1912

The Sound Effects Boy – 1913

'Nearly Midnight Before We'd Finish'

It was 1913 and I was working at Rooney's Saw-mill during the day for seven bob a week. I was thirteen, and not going to school since I come to Australia when I lost my father. And at night I worked at the picture show as Sound Effects Boy. For which I got one and six a week. The Stanley Theatre was in Stanley Street by Lowth's Hotel.[11] It was on a quarter-acre block, and it had no roof on and it had about a fifteen-foot corrugated-iron wall round it. George Page was the manager.

And it had the stage which was a platform at the bottom end of the allotment built on three-b'-twos. The allotment was asphalted and there were rows of canvas chairs. The operating-box was up near The Gods which was a big set of stairs at the back. And under that was a suction gas-producer and a nine inch cylinder, five-foot fly-wheel, ten horsepower, horizontal engine, belt-driven to a hundred and ten volt sixty amp, sixty

---

11   Lowth's Hotel had been built by Tom Lowth in 1897. The original building had an awning decorated with classical pilasters, and balisters replacing the more usual iron-lace of the verandahs. In 1910, in keeping with the tradition of theatres being associated with hotels, Lowth, Thomas Page and C.R. Wood formed Stanley Pictures Ltd, built an open-air theatre behind the hotel in Stanley Street for showing silent movies, then a novelty.

11aPresumably meaning 'with a blow-lamp'.

volt generator. You used to have to blow on it[11a] to start. At seven o'clock I had to turn up and arm the fuser making the methane gas, when the engine-driver, Hughie Woods would start the engine. And then the lights went up and the big carbon-arc at Lowth's Hotel lit up because it was wired to it; that was our big light. And then the flying-ants come round the light. The boarders at Lowth's couldn't live with it because of the flying-ants. And when I'd got the engine going I cleaned m'hands and went backstage.

By this time the customers were coming in. So he'd gimme some change and me lolly-tray and I'd 'Lollies and chocolates!' until the lights went out. Toblers' Chocolate, for threepence, and McIntoshes' Toffees, threepence a tin. I used to pinch 'em out and eat 'em! And put a bit of programme back in to stop 'em rattling! For which I got two bob a week. And the cigarettes were called 'My Darling' and they were about as thick as a pencil and had a gold paper band on the end of them. It was scented tobacco, and they were for the ladies. Two whiffs and a draw and they're gone. You wouldn't get a smoke out of them! It wasn't respectable for girls to smoke. It was only for the girls down the Lane. Even young fellows didn't smoke that much. And pipes, they were just for stinking old men! Smell them a mile off!

The stage at the front was framed with embossed metal. The curtain was on ropes hauled up by a wooden windlass. And there was an advertisement curtain artistically painted with 'Garbutts - Always on Top!' or 'Horn and Petersons', 'Cathcart and Richie - Plumbers' and about forty others.

Then when the show was to start, Hughie Williams would let down the white screen which was on pulleys, and pull it tight with horse-harness buckles, and it was my job to wind up the advertisement curtain. Then when the show was about to start I'd go round the back and make sure my sound effects was all there, and wait until Bill Guy on the piano started up with 'Gawd Save.'[12]

In the enclosure was an operating box which had one Gorman Graphic projector operated by Mr. Honey Goodman who was an electrician by trade. When one spool of film was run out, he would put a slide on the screen saying 'Just a moment please till the operator changes reels'. This would start all the young blokes booing and yelling, 'Hurry up, Honey! Get off your coit!' This would happen about ten times a night. The projector didn't have a motor on it. Electric motors were not very common in those days. It had a handle he turned, so if he was in a hurry to finish for the night you had to concentrate to get your money's worth.

I would sit on my chair and look at the programme and there would be about five pictures, generally one scenic, one educational, two slap-sticks and one drama, or a blood-and-guts Cowboys and Indians one. All Silents, of course. Some had two titles, like *Wander the Earth* or *The Power of Love.* In the scenic one I would get some sleep because I was worn out, and then work through the rest. We used to get the programme sent to us a week ahead, that's if it didn't get held up in the mails. And then you knew what the sound-effects were going

---

12   Until the mid-1950s, all performances of theatre, film, etc., were preceded by the playing of the national anthem, God Save the King' (or Queen).

to be for that picture. The programme would give me a rough idea of what I would need. And the captions told me a lot. I had to be fast reading them because from the back of the screen the captions were backwards to me. The compositor at the *Bulletin* used to laugh because I could read the print-blocks backwards as fast as he could. On the table in front of me was a sheet of corrugated iron about ten feet long to make a bench, and there were two chairs because sometimes it needed two sound-effects boys. I got paid but the other bloke got nothing because he was learning the job. Piggy Bean, he was; he'd be about the same age as me. I get one-and-six for doing it but he gets nothing. He works there just to see the pictures. Poor Piggy, he was a bit light on. We had a half a cask and I used to 'Boom! Boom! Boom!' on it for the Indians. And Piggy used to dance round, and he'd be going 'Woo! Woo! Woo!' for the Indians. He loved it! He used to sell newspapers down on Lowth's Corner, during the day time.

Now for the sound effects, you made up your own. For the railway engine I had two wire brushes and you had a kerosene tin punched upwards with a nail and then you scratched that with the brushes. 'Dooff! Dooff! Dooff!'. For a fist-fight you had an old sulky-seat and two sticks. And if a cowboy hits another cowboy, you whacked the pad. "Voomph! Voomph!'

The gun noises was done with a butter-box. Butter came in 'em. Beautiful boxes. And they were about twelve inches square, made of good timber, and we had two of them, and you bang the lids down, and it made a noise like the gun, near enough. Cowboys and Indians were the favourites. When they're making them the guns were loaded with face-powder so when they're fighting the smoke comes out the barrel. And I slam the boxes down to make the sound.

And then for horses on a road, you had the two coconut shells on an old wash-stand. And you 'clockitty clock, clockitty clock'. And then for a typewriter you had this big morse-key. And then we had bells, for a school ma'am and all that, and a gong which I thieved out of a boxing-ring, and all sorts of car-horns, and whistles, for boats and all. For a fire we had penny-rulers on the bench and you turn this roller and it clicked them – like the cracking of a fire. Then there was the roller for making the waterfall, which was a galvanized iron drum, half-full of pebbles. You turned that, and it made the sound of water. And then for thunder you had a sheet of iron hanging up and you shake it.

So if you got a picture and it's a train full of cowboys shooting a mob of Indians on horses going over a bridge near a waterfall with a bushfire in the background and a fist-fight on the foot-plate! You were moving! You've got the shot-boxes going, the Cowboys and Indians fighting, and I'm belting the pad, and you got to keep the waterfall going, and somebody's got to keep the engine going! The engine's got to be going all the time! You're half mad by the time you're finished. If you go wrong you get your arse kicked off by old George Page. He'd yell, 'You're messing all the show!' You worked! This is at the age of thirteen!

And this night, Old George Page come down and he's flapping the programme and he said, 'Look at this! We've got a big gun here! There's a big gun coming!' he said. 'So what can you do?' So I gets a lump of four-b'-two, and we brang it down on the stage. And she goes with a wallop. Bang! And he said, 'That'll do!' So, this night, it was in the Crimean War and it's the hero bloke, a good-looker. He's a gunner and he pulls a lanyard to set the gun off and the gun bucks and breaks his leg and he's sent home to his sheila.

Well, anyway, I've got this bit of four-b'-two up on the rope, see, and we're waiting to see this gun go off – you see all this face-powder and stuff coming out the gun for the smoke, and Piggy Bean, he's watching the screen and he's saying, I'll tell you! I'll tell you!'. And he says, 'Right!' And the gun goes off so I fetch this lump of timber down with a thump! And it lands right on Piggy's bloody foot! Well, he lets out a yell, and around the stage he's going! And he's yelling blue murder! And the crowd are roaring laughing. It's like this gunner bloke in the picture is doing the squealing, getting his bloody leg broken! And old George Page come up and didn't he boot me up the backside for messing up the picture! That was *The Big Gun*!

You never relaxed in a good picture. You didn't have time. But in a love-story, where they just made love, you could put your two feet on the table and snore. Then you got a drama. Viola Negri was one of the women; and Freda Vara. Freda Vara was a beautiful girl. She had a head of hair, black! And eyes done up! She was my favourite! And when they were having a bad temper, or having a row with their boyfriend, ooh! They'd.........! with their eyes! And the camera would pan on to their faces!

The orchestra used to give you a hand. If there was plenty of rifles well, the drummer would come in with the drum. If it was a martial picture, he would give the soldiers marching with the kettle-drum. And then the cornet would take up the bugle and he'd blow the 'Charge!' The orchestra was half your effects.

The orchestra had jobs during the daytime and they'd get a few shillings at night doing the pictures. But Bill Guy, it was his living, because he composed music. If I wanted to do a song, I'd whistle it to him and he'd write it down and charge me two bob. Hand-written music, that's how he made a quid. We had Bill Guy on the piano, and a big base-fiddle, 'dumph, dumph, dumph', and a bloke on the drums. And we had an old beat-up drunk playing the cornet, then he'd do the bugle act for battles. Then we had the violin. If there was a sad bit in the picture they used to catch on quick. The first night was bad. The second night was good. The orchestra seen it from the front. I'm looking from the back of the screen! No practice, no nothing. The pianist, he knew a song for everything. And if there was a bloke putting the hard word on a sheila he'd play *The Gypsy's Warning* – 'Do not trust him, Gentle Maiden...'! Everyone knew what *The Gypsy's Warning* was!

And we got horror pictures. Bello Lucosi, he was the bad bugger. He was a scientist and they had all these machines and they were whirring. It was really hair-raising. You didn't know what sort of noises to make when you seen them! You'd hit anything! You had them all going! So what with having to compete with a five-piece orchestra going flat out, and the audience yelling their guts out, by the time the hero was kissing the sheila at the end of a two-reeler we were all buggered: audience, orchestra, and sound-effects boy and all, as well as the projectionist who got carried away with the excitement and turned the handle like hell! If you did a good job on the sound effects, they'd give you a clap. If they started laughing there was something wrong!

The blackfellas would get in for nothing. If they liked the picture they'd stay. If they didn't they'd go out half way through. And this night there was a blackfella come in and he was from beyond the Stump. The picture was Fatty Arbuckle, and Fatty's getting chased by a farmer, and he gets in the haystack. And the farmer's poking this pitch-fork into the haystack. And the blackfella yells out, 'Look-out! Boss! 'E stick yu long arse-hole long yu!'

I earned my one-and-six a week! And if it looked like rain we had to put the chairs back under the side before we could go home. And it would be getting on for midnight before we'd finish.

Lowth's Hotel with an advertisement for Stanley Pictures on the railing. Silent movies were shown in an open-air area fenced with corrugated iron behind the hotel. Joe Clark worked there as the sound-effect boy for one-and-six ((18ₑ) a week.

And Harry Houdini came.[13] He booked the theatre. And I give him a hand to shift the junk off the stage. And he's going to jump into a tank of water, with a straight-jacket, a loony-suit. Anyhow, he gets on the top of the proscenium and he jumps into this bloody tank and the tank busted. When he hit the tank the rivets carried away and water went everywhere. The

13   Harry Houdini was an American escape artist and conjurer who attained fame by his escapes from ropes and handcuffs, from trunks under water and strait-jackets.

audience got wet. So next night they got iron bands and they put round the tank, and they filled the tank up, and when he jumps in half the bloody water goes out, and he's standing up to his middle in water without taking this straight-jacket thing off!

That was Houdini. He kicked my backside! He had this mail-bag trick, a simple thing, but it looks good from the audience. The sack, a big sack, made of canvas. And he gets in it, and – I don't know whether it was Mrs. Houdini, but he had a dame – she holds the sack while someone from the audience would tie the rope round, makes sure he can't get out of this one, sort of thing. Then they drop this curtain, so that people won't be able to see how he gets out. And then they lift the curtain and here he is, he's out the sack and he's got this rope he's been tied in with and he's waving it round.

But I seen what they did. I seen the gear in the daytime. And he had a bolster, made of sacking, all rolled up, and when he got in the sack he put the bolster up here, and then his wife put the bag round the bolster, and you tied it as hard as buggery, but he pulls the bolster out, see! Then he takes the rope off and jumps out the sack! He's out the sack as fast as that, see!

Of course, I tell him how the trick's done, and he booted my back-side for me! I knew how it was done! I seen this bolster!

He was a peculiar man. He had a very protruding forehead. And he was always serious. He's walking round and he's making sure a buckle will unbuckle, undoing it, making sure that the gear ran. And when he walked, he didn't walk, he bounced along. He was on the ball on his toes, like an orang-outang! He was tense. A good showman, but he was under a strain.

Entertainments

STANLEY PICTURES

Continued success attended the new management's efforts at the Stanley last night, when a fine audience was present. A feature of the bill are the very charming illustrated songs contributed by Miss Tessie Phelan, who is a singer of decided merit. Her songs were again enthusiastically encored. "Love is stronger than gold" is a drama of unusual power and originality, and other pictures to be selected from a bright programme were "Treasure Island" a story of the sea, and "The Mystery of Room 99" backed by a strong array of comics and scenic subjects.

ROYAL PICTURES

Kovarick had another great reception at the Royal last night. He is a violinist with a good reputation and has established his name very securely in Townsville. His exquisite playing again evoked prolonged applause. "Shanghaied", one of the most exciting and thrilling sea dramas ever screened, made a big hit. It is a fine glimpse of the deeds of the men "who dare things" and possesses a captivating love interest. "Professor Stout's Honeymoon", depicting the trials and tribulations usually not connected with this happy function was one long peal of merriment. Other dramas and comics (all "top-notchers") completed a singularly good bill, which will be presented for the last time to-night.

JONES' I.X.L. JAMS made from pure Tasmanian fruit are unequalled throughout Australia and Tasmania.

And the Barrymores were here. They were working for the Phillip Lytton dramatic company, which only showed drama, *East Lynn* and all that. You got *East Lynn* until you got sick of it. And one time, J.C. Williamson was coming and he booked the theatre for a week. The show's called *Are You a Mason?* So Old George Page tells me to hire a billy-goat to help with the advertising. Well, there was goats all over the hill but they're not going to let me lay a hand on them, are they! Townsville was full of goats and I had a mate, he lived behind the brewery. He had this racing-goat called Stinky Poo. I went and looked him up and he said I could have Stinky Poo for a bob.

But this goat he wasn't called Stinky Poo for nothing! Talk about on the honk! So I clean him up with a good bath. He did a bit of resisting! And I painted his horns – he had these flamin' great corkscrew horns – and I painted 'em with red stripes, like a barber's pole. And I took him to the Stanley. And George Page had got this flannel coat made up for him, and it had *Are You a Mason?* on it. And he'd also got a square of tin with a compass painted on it to hang round his neck. And he had this long velvet coat for me to put on, and it's got the compass on the back and the front.[14]

So Saturday morning, at half-past eleven, just when Flinders Street is going to be packed out, off I go leading Stinky Poo on this halter. I'm supposed to start from the bottom end of Flinders Street, head up to the Post Office, then on up Denham

---

14   It was a widely held belief among Townsville children as late as the 1940s that members of the Masonic Lodge in Sturt Street rode billy-goats at midnight on the adjacent block of vacant land. The 'compass' was part of the Masonic insignia.

Street, and back round Sturt Street to the Salvation Army, then back into Flinders Street.

Well, me and Stinky Poo just stopped the town! All the kids was following us. The buses pulled up to let us through! Everybody's laughing and yelling out, 'Which one is Stinky Poo?' and 'Are you off to join the Lodge, Joe?'

And we get down a bit, near Hayles', and Stinky Poo gets sight of a nanny-goat, and he's 'Snort! Bruughh!' and bucking around and trying to break loose! And everyone's killing themselves, and all the kids is following, and the nanny-goats bringing up the rear! Even Stanley Green[15] the editor of the *Bulletin* come out and had a laugh! (He didn't give us any free ads, but!) And I get back to the Stanley Theatre and I go to tie old Stinky Poo up to the door but he's had enough! He puts his head down and gives a bit of a buck and he backs out of the halter and takes off up Castle Hill. He's still got this flannel coat on! And the nanny-goat's close behind him! Anyhow, it done the trick as an advertising stunt. We had a full house all week! That was *Are You a Mason?*

Then you got another company – *On Our Selection, Dad and Dave.* Oh, they were good! Because you knew what they were doing, and they could make it funny! And Dave, he's got a loaf of bread and he's going to carve it up, and he's thinking about how he can get Mabel to come down and look at the new fence, and forgets, and he scratches his backside with the bread! Well, that brought the house down!

---

15   Possibly David Green who had previously been editor of the *Norlh Queensland Register.*

And Harry Clay come. And he used to run a singing competition and I always won it. See, they'd go by the clapping. Who got the most clapping won. And everybody knew me, and the most claps was always for Joe! And I'd get five shillings for me Mum!

Townsville Railway Station, about 1912, with horse-drawn cabs waiting for customers.

The Little Battler – 1913

'Anything to Make a Quid'

When I was a boy, we worked eight and a half hours, and then from eight till half-past twelve on Saturday. That was our working week.

Well, us poor people, what you got for breakfast was what you had for dinner last night. If there was any stew left over, well you had stew on bread in the morning. That'd be your breakfast. It was the best you could do. Mince on toast was a favourite, if you'd been having mince the night before. If you had fowls you had eggs. We always had fowls. We had tons of eggs. Then sometimes you'd have fried bread. It was called German toast, just fried in the fat. But you had to use up and be economical on food, see.

We never heard the word 'vitamins' but you knew that you had to eat so much meat, and you had to have so much milk. And vegetables. Your mother knew that you had to have the right food. We come up healthy.

Your dinner was what your mother made. She would cut up potatoes and put them between bread. You filled yourself. You eat that and you had a billycan and you made your tea at the place and then you worked in the afternoon till five o'clock.

And everybody had goats. They kept the gutters clean, lolly-papers, mangoes – there was not a thing that the ants could get when a goat's about. The goats ate the bloody lot! My mother had goats. We lived on goats' milk. You've got to get the taste, but it's not bad. We used to catch a goat in the street and milk her. Catch 'em anywhere! They 'Baaa!' like bloody-hell, and you hold its nose while you're milking them! Get the milk and let her go, and the old woman that owned her never got any milk that night!

Townsville Railway Station under construction, 1913.

A bloke, Paddy Sabadeen, him and me milked a goat one day, and we drank the milk on the spot. Paddy wasn't fond of hot milk, but I didn't mind; milk's milk to me. And this old woman, she got hold of Paddy, and she give him a tongue-bashing. And Paddy, he had some funny answers. 'Bloody Hell, Joe!' he said, 'I wasn't milking her! I was milking the bloody goat!'

Some people called the male goat a stinker. We called it a snob. He used to 'Brrugh! Brrrugh!' and fart, and snort, and piss all over himself! And he had long horns, and he'd have you on, you know! Oh, yes! Put his head down and go for you! Some was tame of course. But when we seen a courting' couple, we'd 'Brrrugh! Bruuugh!' and get our arse kicked!

When the water-melon season was on we'd go into a

Chinaman's shop, and he kept all the water-melons on this side of the counter, see. And one bloke'd say he wanted a packet of cigarettes, and while the Chinaman turned his back I'd be rolling the melons out with m' bare-foot! And m'mate outside catching them! They were only worth threepence a melon, you know.

And down in Flinders Lane, there were opium dens. It would be like a fernery, you go in and there's shelves like wooden benches and there'd be old Ah Fats snoring there, lying there knocked, with only a rice bag opened up for a cover. And they had a funny pillow, the Chinaman, a wooden one. I tried to pinch one because it was beautiful job! A piece o' hard-wood and it was carved with different recesses and when he would sleep on his side he would turn the pillow and get his ear on to it, and on the back he'd put the pillow under his neck and sleep that way. There was a handle on the block and, my word, he would fell you with it if you got in his road, see! They were all sleeping and us kids we were right through because we were looking for opium tins!

They'd sneak this opium in over the coast and it was in these flat tins. They reckon the *Chang Ti*[16] used to throw it over on a buoy and someone would go out and pick it up. One fellow had a boat called the *Red Wing*. He got caught. They took his boat and he went to prison. The opium come in tins, flat oval; and it would be about six or eight inches long, and it would be four inches across. And when they'd finished with 'em they'd chuck 'em away and us kids'd be after them. They

---

16   Possibly the 'Changsha' which made regular visits to the port of Townsville from Hong Kong

was worth money! And then when you opened it up you got a sheet of brass. And it was imprinted on the brass, in Chinese, 'Rod Kee and Co. Canton'. And the plumbers used to buy them off us, threepence a tin! And they'd open them up and make spectacle-cases, the sort that you put the spectacles in the end. When we found a tin we took it down the creek to wash it out. You couldn't take it home because it had this smell. A sort of smell that never lets you up. And I'd wash 'em in the creek because if I took 'em home they'd smell around the house. And Mum would have been on to me! And in the creek the fish'd be lying belly upwards where you washed 'em!

All the kids were after them. You were lucky to get a few, if you got down early when they was cleaning up. Threepence would buy a double-ice-cream; threepence would pay for a pie! With peas and potatoes! So threepence was something! You never told your mother about them sort of threepences you got! She didn't like you doing it so we never told her!

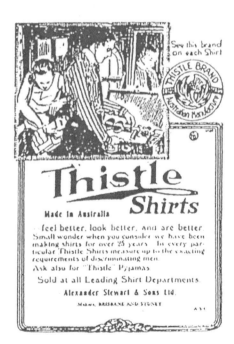

The young Chinese never took opium on. Only the old fellows who'd come out. There was a lot of Chinese come in on the side. They used to jump off the *Chang Ti* and swim ashore, and the local Chinese would work 'em to death in the gardens. Some parts of Mysterton Estate, that was all Chinese, running round with their buckets. They never spoke to nobody but they worked like horses.

If they had to take an oath in court, well, the translation of it was, 'If I tell lies may my soul be dashed to pieces as this dish', and then they'd break a dish. If it didn't break they'd do it again. And one old chap he did it again and it still didn't break. And again. So he jumped on it. And he's saying, 'Lallikin! (that means 'larrikin', see) Damn! Fart!' (Some kid would have told him. The kids used to torment the life out of them.)

You would go out to Hermit Park from town, and where the Catholic church is, St. Mary's, on that side, that was the Cummins' Estate, and then there was the Roberts' Estate, and further on, the land dipped down away from the road into a gully. That was all Chinamen's gardens.

For water, they had a well, and a pipe down the well, and a Californian pump, which was a piece of chain that went round, and wooden disks bolted on the chain. And on the wheel at the top was a horse, and he kept walking round, stepping over the shafts all the time, and all these wooden disks carried the water up, and then it tipped over in the chute, and then the Chinaman was there, and he's backed up with his yoke and his two tins. Then he toddled away and he watered a row, and then he's straight back. And, all day they did that. Yes, there was a lot of the Chinese. And you could go and get threepence worth of shallots, threepence worth of lettuce. They only charged threepence a bunch for everything. Carrots and turnips. Chinee cabbage. But they were good to deal with. Honest. More than a white man.

And Chinese New Year is not our New Year. Chinese New Year is about between January and February. And the Chinamen always paid their debts. No Chinaman was in debt over a year. And Chinese New Year he made his trip to anywhere you like but he paid his debts. And there was no English fireworks. Only Chinese. So you buy your fireworks at the Chinaman's. And Chinese New Year they used to put them on the Strand and give us a show. They'd have crackers banging there right through the night on the Strand, on Chinese New Year. They never cared what they spent.

And in those days everybody was poor. So when a funeral was on, there was no putting it in the paper. The undertaker had little squares of paper, edged in black and he'd go round and tack these on the telegraph-poles. If you wanted to know who'd died you'd go round the posts and see. There was nothing in the paper. That cost money!

And Charlie Burns and me, one time there, our mothers wanted some paper-bark to do fern-baskets. So him and me we go out the Common. And the funerals used to come in on the Common side. Anyhow, we get this paper-bark, and it's full of ants. You carry paper-bark on a string, you don't carry it on your shoulder 'cause it will make you lousy, see. And we've got these lumps of paper-bark and we're walking back and the arse falls out of the clouds! And, Boy! Geez, it come down. And we seen the hearse coming and George Crowe, he's driving. He's taken somebody out and he's coming back. And we go, 'Give us a ride!' And he's sitting himself on the top of the glass wagon in the rain with a mac. on. He says, 'Git in the back!' So we open the glass doors and we're sitting in the back! And we're hanging on to the rails, bouncing round. And we're bangin' on the roof trying to let him know to let us out! But he drives us right up to Mum's place! And everybody has a good geek at Joe and Charlie in the glass wagon!

And I was working in McConnel's Plumbing Shop as odd-job boy. Eight and a half hours a day and from eight until half-past twelve on Saturday. That was our working week. Seven bob a week. I'd have been maybe fourteen. Old McConnel was an Irishman and as mean as cat-shit. A bugger of a boss. He was nothing, but he engaged the plumbers. There was Jack Reid; he was the tinsmith on the bench in the shop. There was Bolger Mercer with a boy. He was a water-plumber; that was a speciality. They used to make lead joints and that. Charlie Mays was the glazier. There'd be seven or eight of us. I was helping to put roofs on. We'd take the iron out in the spring-cart. It was a soldering job. I used to like that.

And taking a stove out, and putting a stove in. But the cunning old bugger, McConnel, he used to send me out at five o'clock with the stoves. We had an old horse and a spring-cart, and he'd yell, 'Here, Joe! Put this stove in the cart and take it out to Hermit Park.' Well, you wouldn't get there by five! By the time you got it out and shoved this stove in the house, get a hand where you could, maybe assemble it, it'd be dark! Then back again and feed the horse and water the horse and walk home. On a kid it's a lot! And this old bugger used to keep on doing this! And at five to five I used to run away, get in the lavatory, but get out of his way, because there's a stove going! See! He was bad!

But I got square on him. I overfed his horse. Instead of giving him one bucket of chaff I used to give him one bucket of chaff and one scoop of corn. And I loaded him up with it. The bugger! I'd fill his horse up! In the end the horse couldn't walk! And the feed bill went up! I went through hell about that!

And we made billy-cans in our spare time. You couldn't just do nothing or you'd get the sack. And Old Mac used to hang them on the ceiling on a rope. One day I was cleaning up, sweeping the floor, and Mac was in the shop, and a swaggie come along. He come to the door. Now a swaggie is a poor man. He's got nothing. And he looks in at the door and he says, 'Hey, Son! Is there an old tin I can have for a billy-can?' And all these new billies are hanging up. They're for stock, see.

Old Mac isn't around, so I get the hook and I take them down. The rope breaks! And they all fall! And I grabbed a billy and I shied it through m'legs and the swaggie caught it and he off! Mac comes in and he gives a yell. 'What the bloody hell's going on!'

And I'm going crook about 'yer bloody rope just broke!', see, to try and get meself off the hook!

And he says, 'Yairs! An' there was twelve billy-cans there, and there's only eleven there now! Who's got the other one?'

And I'm going, 'I haven't got your bloody billy!' But the swaggie had gone. And he didn't know that. McConnel took ninepence out of my pay for that!

And the *Bulletin* office was in the same block, two doors up. And, of course, kids are everywhere, so I used to go up the *Bulletin* and watch the suction-gas job engine driving the printing machine. And at the back of the *Bulletin* office was a place called the stereo17. It was where they cast the rollers, the type-metal rollers, and it was where they made up the flong. Flong is mat. You've got six sheets of blotting paper, and five sheets of tissue paper, and then you've got a sheet of cardboard that big, or bigger, and a cast-iron slab. And you paint it with the

---

17   (Macquarie Dictionary) stereotype; a method of producing cast metal printing plates from a mould made from a form of type.

swab brush. And you put the first piece of tissue-paper down and then you put the first piece of very thin blotting paper. And you roll it. And squeeze all the rubbish out. Then you put the tissue on and you put the paste on, and you roll that, see. And in the end you've got a mat which is called a flong. And then the type-metal was put in the frame and the flong was put on top and the whole lot shoved in the roller. And it pushed the whole impression into the flong. And then the flong was taken off, and there was the imprint of today's paper.

And that flong then was put in the mould, and when they poured the lead in then it become the print rollers, when they printed the *Bulletin*. And I used to go, in my dinner-hour – I wouldn't get any dinner, or I'd eat it on the job, bread and dripping or bread and syrup – I'd nick up the *Bulletin*, and I used to go up and make flong. A half-penny a sheet you got for making this. A half-penny, that's less than half a cent.

And I might knock up four pieces of flong in my dinner-hour. The man would sign, 'Give Joe tuppence' and I'd take this to Head Office and get tuppence. And I'd made tuppence for Mum, see. We were broke. Hard up all the time. I'd do anything to make a quid. We had to eat!

I even jumped in – Remember Jimmy Sharman? Well, his father or grandfather came up here with this fighting mob. A travelling Boxing Tent. And I was knocking round with some fellows. We used to call ourselves the Boomerang Gang. We had these boomerangs, a penny. And we didn't pay to go in the Show Grounds. We used to nick down near the keeper's house and hop the fence. Never paid a shilling to get into the Show Grounds!

So Jimmy Sharman has got a little weed of a kid. 'Any weights on to fight this fellow?' It was just an attraction before the big fight. And I sang out,

'I could bloody eat him!' And I can't fight my way out of a wet paper bag!

And he said, 'You want to have a go?' And I said, 'How much for?'

And he says, 'Ten bob if you're still on your feet in four rounds!'

He chucks me the gloves and my gang say, 'Are you goin' to have a go?'

And I say, 'Yeah! I'll bloody kill him!' And I'm thinking, 'Oh, Gawd! What did I say that for!'

And Fatty Maclaren said, 'I'll bet you two bob he licks you!'

And I says, 'Right! I'll bet youse all two bob!' And I haven't got two bob!

So they says, 'Righto! You're on!'

And in I go, and of course, there was lots of people knew I was 'Little Joe.' They knew I didn't have a father and I was fighting for the ten bob! So I get in the ring and we're dancing round like a pair of cocks for a while. And he comes in and he makes one hell of a swing at me, and I put me guard up and he, 'Bang!', gets me on the ribs. Christ! He nearly folded me up.

Anyhow, Jimmy Sharman – we was supposed to fight two-minutes. If anyone's getting a hiding he just rings a bell, see. And somebody's told Jimmy that I needed the money. So, Artie Olsen, was a footballer, he come in and he's got the towel fanning me, in me corner. Nobody's fanning the other kid. He's tough! Anyway, Artie Olsen says, 'Joe! You want to git outa this! He'll kill yer!'

I said, 'I'll git one on him!'

He said, 'No chance! You can't git near 'im!'

Now it's coming on, and we git in again, and it's 'Bang!' And in the end, I'm coming in sideways! I'm folded up! And Artie Olsen says, 'Joe! The only chance you got of being with 'im at the end is to get round his bloody neck and stop there! Less you won't be on your bloody feet to git your ten bob!'

Anyway, I get round his bloody neck and I stuck tight. He couldn't shift me off! And in the end they pull the bell and I get me ten bob and I go out. And I had a shirtful of sore ribs. But I got me ten bob and I get me two bob each off four of the gang! And I took the money home to Mum. We needed the money! We were poor! But so was everybody else! But I had to battle for mine!

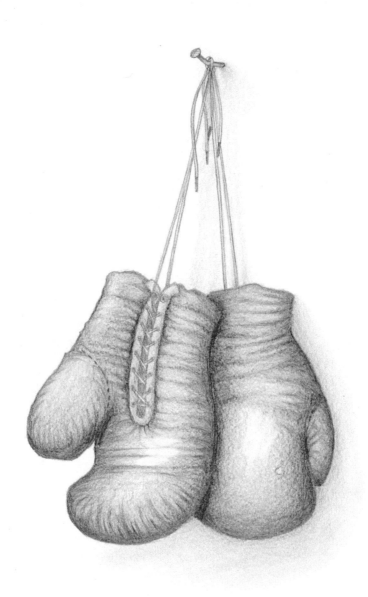

The Water Joey – 1914

'Nippering on the Line'

I heard that they were building a railway line from Nome to Alligator Creek and I walked out from Townsville. I wanted a job with more money than I was getting at the saw-mill. And that would be six miles to Stuart's Creek and another five it would be to Nome.

And I get there at five in the afternoon. I walked all day. I was sunburnt to buggery. I had two odd sand-shoes on and a sixpenny 'pick o' the basket' straw hat. See, straw hats was in. Well, then, when a straw hat was kept in the shop too long it went yellow. So they're put in a basket out the door, and your mother would bring you along and you'd stick one on and walk in and give him the zack. See! Sixpenny 'pick o' the basket'! That was my hat! I'd have been thirteen years old, going on fourteen.

And I started there nippering. My job was to carry water for the navvies working on the line, the Water Joey. The line started at Nome. Behind the station was a rolling-machine for bending the curves. Then there was a galley and a store-room. The galley had a wood-stove in. It was a tent and the store-room was a shed. Alongside of that were the huts for the boss and the cook, and the men were camped in tents on the flat, between the railway-station and the river – a bit of a creek it was. The tents were supplied by the meatworks.

They cut down the saplings and made the tents. The men did mine. I was a Pommy and couldn't do it! Didn't know how! I got 'Pommy' all the time. You were a 'Pommy Bastard' to start. But when the Australian accepted you he called you 'Chum'. You see, I was a New Chum. But I never got 'Chum' until I earned it. Later on, you got, 'Hey! Chum! How you going?' So the men did my tent and the fly because I was a New Chum. The tent's to live in. And the fly goes over it. As long as nobody's touching the fly it won't leak. The rain follows the fly down and gets off. Every two men had a ten-by-eight.

A Fettlers' camp like the one at Nome where Joe signed on as 'Nipper', or water-joey in 1914. The men erected his tent because he was 'new-chum'.

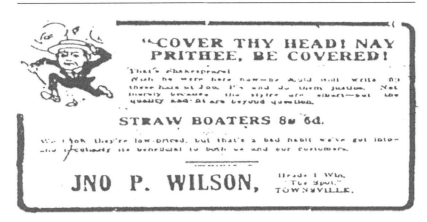

You had your own lamp. A hurricane. You buy that. They're not going to give you that. They gave you two stretchers – stretcher-beds. They were made in Rooney's Sawmill. Sawn timber, the one that folds the legs underneath. Alligator Creek had them by the thousands! You had to find your own swag. We used to get sacks, corn sacks, potato-bags, and you put newspaper in them. No pillow. You used your boots! You stand your boots up and your ear fits in the boot and you sleep like that.

The river didn't run, but they put a pipe-case in the bed with no bottom in, and made a well, and good sweet water came in, and the cooks used that for the cooking. My job was to carry the water. And I carried it in a kerosene tin on m'shoulder, which was forty-pounds. That's ten pound a gallon. And I had a piece of pine about seven inches square on top of the water so that I could carry it on my shoulder without it splashing out. And then I'd walk the sleepers. I was an expert at stepping on the sleepers. Because the land was all broken up alongside of it with the horse-scoops. So I was the water boy and I took the water to the navvies.

Railway 'pumpers' or trolleys, of two kinds. Those on which the linesmen are sittling astride were worked by pushing like handles backwards and forward. The flat-topped kind were used for transporting the "gang", and had a vertical handle which two men, standing opposite one another, worked up and down like as ship's pump.

Cyril Abrahams came out every Friday with the cheques, on a horse. And we could walk to Alligator Creek and catch Hayles' Ferry in on the Saturday dinnertime, to come home, because if you wanted to come home you did, and if you didn't you stopped there; the food went on. In my case I'd come back once a fortnight to give Mum the two cheques. But it was no use spending money with Bob Hayles every week. You're wasting money, sort of thing, see! And you had to walk four miles from Nome to Alligator Creek to get the boat. It was just as easy to sit in the bush.

And a chap named Kelly O'Halloran he was the Spike Boy. He carried the spikes on a plank, carried them right up, same as I carried the water. And a boy named Emil Birril was the Marker-Off Boy. He was at the head of the show, of us boys. And when they took the sleepers and the rails up the top end, he had two pieces of stick and a piece of chalk, and he marked from the end of the sleeper with his chalk and that was where the rail would lie. And then he'd kick the sleepers into position for roughly the spacing.

Every morning the train came out from Townsville with the supplies, food, and a couple of newspapers and mail. Alligator Creek sent a lot of meat too. And with the train came Mr A.E. Frew, a local man, the engineer for the line.[18]

The train backed up the line with the wagons first and unloaded the sleepers and the rails as far as they could go on the made line. And we had a half a thousand-gallon tank and he would fill that from a water-gin, that is, a water-wagon, for us to use. We couldn't come right back to the camp to get water. So that five-hundred gallon, open tank was filled from the gin, for me to give to the men.

And then the train would go. Then Jack Snell, he had a horse named Paddy, and a plate-laying trolley. Which was a flat affair, with sides about six inches higher than the body. And the rails lay along the trolley between the sides and the sleepers lay on the sides. Well, they would go right to the head of the rails, where they're laying the rails. Well, two navvies would take these sleepers, one at a time, one at each end of them, and chuck them out on the permanent-way, which was already made by men with horse-scoops. No dozers in them days!

And they would lay these sleepers out as near as they could and then Jim McKirgo, a Charters Towers man, he was the plate-laying boss, and he would have a rope. Which he put a half-hitch round one rail. And the men took that rope way ahead of the sleepers they'd laid, and they ran. And when he yelled they let go of everything and that rail would drop on to the sleepers.

---

18   A.E. Frew was the leading railway contractor in North Queensland for twenty years.

Then he'd come back and half-hitch another one. And that would be pulled out, and dropped. And that was your rail on top of the sleepers, which Emil Birril in the meantime had marked with his chalk. And then the gang come along with the jiggers, that's the borer, and bored the holes and drove the spikes and there's another length of rail down.

And then the plate-laying trolley moved ahead and done the same thing until there was no more. And then Jack fetched the horse back and loaded up again, see. And all this time I'm going backwards and forwards with the bucket. Because they're getting away from me! I'm going backwards and forwards with the bucket to keep the water up to them because, by God, they were thirsty! They're all Pommies! Englishmen, Irishmen, all as red as crabs! And a few Swedes. And I was cooked like a prawn! The immigration was only Pommies then. There wasn't many other people came here.

When the train came up it fetched our food. It was very far from the base camp; a good two miles. The food would be put on the train and fetched up and the butter was in the tin with a lid on and they hung that on the branch of a tree. We did the best we could. There was no ice. You'd wrap a wet rag around. A few loaves of bread, tins of jam, bottle of pickles, about ten pound of tea in a tin, and whatever cookies the cook had scrambled together the day before. The cook would be a married man from Townsville. And we had the dinner-time in the bush and we boiled the kerosene-tin to get our tea. A pannikin. Then after lunch, you get going again.

And then we had an ant-proof thing which was the neck

of a bottle – you got a bottle and broke it off at the neck – and you made an iron hook and put it right through the cork. And then the bottle was hanging upside down with some water in there and then the ants couldn't come across it. The bought one had a tin funnel on it, but we used to get the neck of a bottle.

Then, another funny thing. If you've seen a hobble chain of a horse, anyhow, it's got round links, real round links, about four or five. Now if you hang anything on a hobble-chain the ants'll come down two rings, but go no further! I think they get giddy! They come down and they go up again! They won't come down five rings! So we'd hang meat and bread up like that.

To get there, you walked the first half-mile, but that was nothing, but after that we had two pump-trolleys and we had two planks. And we put the two pump-trolleys and we spiked the planks on to the pump-trolleys and we left one end free so when it went around a curve it wouldn't lock. Someone would ride on the pump-trolley and pump like hell, and we'd sit on the planks. And we'd get to where we were going, and pull the pump-trolley off and then come back the same way of a night time. The pump-trolley was often used to get back and bring things if they wanted things.

Towards the end of the day when the line had been laid – the line was like a snake anyway – it was just put down – it had to be straightened, and laid, for tomorrow morning's train! Or the thing'd fall off! And an old fellow by the name of Bob Bellyer – he had an eye like a stinking fish! That's a good eye, when you've got an eye like a stinking fish! Then they all went back then, with crow-bars or whatever they had and pull the line sideways and lift it and pack it, so that it was reasonably straight, and Bob would put his eye down and yell out to them and they'd lift it or drop it or shove it sideways so that tomorrow morning's train wouldn't fall off it. Then later on the train would come along with ballast and fill all the holes up and then make it pretty solid. And then more straightening after that. And we get towards Alligator Creek. No accidents. We carried a blacksmith. The pump-trolley often used to get knocked about and he'd repair it, and fix all the men's gear, and doing picks up[19] as well. It was all pick and shovel, you know.

And Kelly O'Halloran, he was colonial Irish. He was from an Irish family in Australia and he was taught to hate the Englishman. Like a kid would be. He had a face like two mile of bad road. He was an ugly boy of a thing. And he hated me because I was English, that was the only reason. And every time I come near him he'd have a crack at me. And I said, 'One day I'll knock you, Kelly!' And he said, 'You're not as good as that!' And he'd want to fight but I wouldn't be game, see! And the men used to watch this. I think if he'd have started somebody would have took me part. I was only tiny and Kelly was a heavy boy. One of the fellows said to me, 'Him and his bloody big nose! The only time it would be any good would be if it was full of O.P. rum or gold-dust!' That was the value of Kelly's nose!

And when we got to the meatworks they were doing a pipe-track to Alligator Creek from Bentley Weir. So I was Water Joey on that. From Bentley to Alligator Creek was only a two-inch line. It was only a boiling-down meatworks. And they're making a freezing meatworks out of it so they had to

---

19   Sharpening the picks.

have more water and a bigger kill. So we put in about a five or six inch cast-iron line.

And the old two-inch line was laid where we were going, so there was a tap about every half mile. So I was right for me water. I could hump it from there. I didn't have to go back to base camp for water. And then the cook and things was carried on by a dray to where the men were. And we walked back to where we were camped at the weir. Jock Semple was the boss there.

This is before the First World War. They knew the war was coming on that's why the meat-line had to go in.

Alligator Creek Meatworks, about 1917. The lighter berthed at the wharf is possibly the Myall where Joe spent a cold night fishing.

Meatworks Boy – 1914

'You Made Your Own Excitement'

And when we got to the meatworks, these men all got jobs. We were part of the Alligator Creek mob then. And Cordingly[20] he's the boss. And I get a job in his house as a cook's off-sider. And I would be the most awkward kid in the world with dishes, and I break – that blue shiny one with the bridge on – the Willow pattern! A quarter of his whole set I broke in one go! Dropped the lot! The cook, he's an old Scotchman, and he yells, 'Only a bloody Sassenach would do such a thing! Get out of here!' I was bloody unnecessary! They got rid of me!

Anyhow, McKenzie, he was building these works. He was a Yank. And he laughed at me breaking all the dishes. He said, 'I'll get you a job!'

And I said, 'I'll get a job in the meat-works!'

He said, 'Oh, no you don't.' He used to like me – big fellow, he was. See, I was a little orphan kid. Everybody knew about m'father, and us being fairly poor, and all that. Anyhow, he says, 'You're gonna work for me!'

And I says, 'What doin'?'

And he says 'My Telephone Boy!' And so we'd walk round

---

20   *(May, Dawn;* Arctic Regions in a Torrid Zone, *The Ross River Mealworks* 1892-1992). Thomas Cordingly. a major shareholder of North Queensland Meat Export Co., formed in 1889, was also appointed manager. The works had the capacity to process one hundred bullocks and just over a thousand sheep per day. A preserving plant capable of treating fifty bullocks daily was added to the existing boiling down and extract facilities.

the place and we'd, say, watch the concrete gang. There was no cement-mixers! It was all shovel!

And when he'd want to see Cordingly, the boss, the Manager of the place, he'd say, 'Here take that! Get Cordingly!' And he'd scribble a note. I was his runner. See! And to get off the top of the place – it was four storeys high – I'd slide down the bannisters, and I'd run and I'd get Cordingly, and I'd fetch him back. And I'd bugger him up walking back up, because, of course, I could run! 'He'll kill me! The bugger!' he used to say.

Anyway, I was McKenzie's Telephone Boy. Messenger Boy. He'd write something down. 'Here, get that sent off!' And I'd run to the office. I was his runner.

Anyhow, this night, he said, 'You're working tonight. Go down and get your tea.' The tea was in the big galley. And we're working on the top floor, and the men are turning the cement, and it's as cold as buggery, and I'm sleeping on the bloody telephone pole up there. And he said, 'Are you tired?'

And I says 'Yeah!'

And, 'Now wait a while,' he says. 'Do you do fishing? Have you got a line?'

And I says, 'Yeah!'

And he says, 'Well, go and get it; get some bait.' That's a bit of scrag meat off the cook, or something, see. I thought we were going fishing.

'I don't want it.' he said. 'Now you go down and get on the *Myall.* That was a lighter they used to take into town with the meat on, cases of meat. So I go down and sit on the *Myall* and I'm sitting there in the freezing cold catching fish. The only fish I ever caught in m'life! Mostly them bloody catfish. Some used to eat them, but I couldn't stand them. Slimey things.

And I fell asleep on the *Myall* and in the morning, he come down and he, 'Hey! Joe! Where are you!'

And I says, 'I'm here!'

'Catch anything?'

I says, 'Yeah!'

'Bring 'em up here!' And he says, 'I'll take these!' And I say, 'You'll take nothin'! I caught these!'

And he says, 'Give me the fish!' Anyway, he took them up to his house. But that's fair! He was a fine man, McKenzie!

Alligator Creek in the first place was a boiling-down works. They killed the cattle and there was no freezing. As soon as they were killed they were in the pot, getting boiled for corned beef only. That was corned beef in tins. It was all exported overseas. Well, then the war came on and the soldiers ate it all. And they got the dripping off it. And the extract was taken off. We used to pinch the extract. A treacle tin was worth about three quid. And we used to pinch a treacle tin and take it home. We lived on the stuff.

And the preserving room gang, which I was in, started at two o'clock in the morning and I think we worked till one o'clock. And we'd got all our meat in the tins and the thing was cleaned down. We slept then – if you could get a sleep – until two o'clock in the morning again. I got more money there, because in the preserving room, nobody wants that job. So I went to there to get the money. Better than what you could get in town.

And Alligator Meatworks were being built, see. The American idea was the cattle walked right to the top. They climbed this race. They couldn't see anything out of the race. It was just like climbing a hill. So the bullock he went up and he got knocked on the head. Then his head was cut off and his guts was pulled out, his hide was taken off, and by the time the guts was cleaned out and the head was taken off and the brains was taken out and then the hide goes down the chute to the bottom, and the other one is coming down behind him. See, that's how they treated the cattle. It was an American idea. They got killed there and by gravity all the carcasses was coming down and by the time it got to the bottom, the hide was finished and the cattle was finished. But in at Ross River everything was on the level.

And Bob Hayles used to run the ferry service back into town. He had a new launch, the *Magneta*. It was just a small thing. It went to Cairns in the end. And before he pulls up alongside the wharf they chuck the rope on the bollard. And McKenzie was standing at the offices near the wharf. And we're all waiting to get on this new boat. And McKenzie sings out, 'Hey! Mr Hayles! How much you going to charge these men to go to town?'

Hayles says, 'Four shillings!'

And McKenzie says, 'No, you won't!' he takes the rope off the bollard. 'You can't charge 'em four bob! They haven't got that much money!'

So Bob goes down with the tide, see. Then he starts his motor up and he comes up again.

McKenzie says, 'How much? Before you tie up!'

Anyway they kept doing this till Old Bob come down to half-a-crown![21]

And McKenzie says 'What about a boy? How much for a boy?'

And Bob yells back, 'Two-and-six! Same as the men.'

And McKenzie says, 'Like hell! One-and-six! Or you don't come alongside!'

And Bob was mad! He says, 'Don't stand over me, you bastard!'

But McKenzie says, 'I'll belt you outa the bloody way quick!' Oh, he was a giant of a man! He pulled Old Bob into line quick. Old Bob couldn't put it over McKenzie and he knew it. So it was one-and-six for us boys.

And Bob Hayles used to bring the *Magneta* out on a Friday night and take us into town, because the men would be thirsty and they got their pay. And at eleven o'clock at night he'd take them back again. Well, it would be a boat-load of drunks. And Alligator Creek, there's a sandbar across the mouth, and if the sand builds up you can't get across it, only on a very high tide. And this particular night the boat's full of drunks and they're spewing... oh! And it's a nauseating smell and you're slipping on the deck. And we get on the bar and the boat's stuck. And it's rolling. It had a Gardiner Kerosene engine but the fumes went up the pipe so you didn't get that smell on deck. But when we got on the bar, well, he stopped the engine. And the boat's lolling. And Bob comes along and he says to me, 'Hey, Son, give us a hand. I think we can get her off now.' So I go down below and he lights the blow-lamp and I had to go along with the hot

---

21   Two shillings and sixpence, slightly more than half the original price asked.

torch. And the boat's rolling. And the fumes! And I spewed, and it went on the engine. And the smell of that made me spew again. And Bob's spewing his head off and that made me worse.

And anyway, we get her off the bar and into the creek and I come out of the engine-room, and Old Bob, he says, 'Thanks!'

And I say, 'Thanks, be buggered! Is that all I get! Gimme a free trip next time!' Because I'd done this for him, crook and all. Nobody else would of got down there! But he said, 'I give no free trips!' He was that kind. He didn't believe in being generous. He died a wealthy man.

And I wanted to go to America. All boys want to go to America. Every boy wants to travel. If you didn't there's something wrong. Everybody has got to try himself out. Girls aren't like boys. And McKenzie says, 'No, Joe. You got a good country here! What do you want to go to America for?'

I says, 'I read about it in *Popular Mechanics*.'

He says, 'Oh, that's only bloody advertising', he says. He says, 'No, Joe. Don't go to America. It's a hard country. You got a good country here. You live in this one. I know America and I know this place. And this is the better country.' Anyway, I never got there.

Anyhow, I was going to work in the meatworks, and boys were anybody's property. See, if I was in the machine shop now, and I decided to go in the preserving room, all I had to say was, I'll swap you jobs!' And the time-keeper'd change your names on the sheet. And here's his name on our side'. Boys were the property of anybody, so if two boys swapped a job, there's nobody to mind.

So when the contract was finished, us kids was kept on, cleaning up. And McKenzie, he says, 'Hey, Joe! Did you get paid?

I says, 'Yes!'

And I said, 'Two pounds!' That was alot of money, you know. The men were only taking home two and a half quid. Eight and a penny a day the men got. That's eighty cents. A two pound loaf of bread was threepence; enough bread to keep you and your fowls going for a day or more.

Anyway, he says, 'Two quid! Show us it!' So he took it, and he says, 'I'll take this!'

And I says, 'Like buggery you will!'

'I'm gonna give you a big one!' he says, and he off, and he wrote me a cheque for five quid! And he says, 'I won't give you this one back. I'll cancel this one. But you take this. You're worth it.' Well, I was made! I had more money than the men!

That's the sort of man McKenzie was. He was a fine man.

I went to Ross River meat-works after that. I was on the butchers' floor picking out nodules. The beef's all hanging, and the nodule is a hard nodule in the hip. Every bullock has got it. It's like a fried egg. And you flick it out. And I'm getting a shilling a bucket for flicking nodules out. And I'm thinking I'm getting a fully-fledged meat-worker!

And down in Flinders Lane, as is Ogden Street now, the Chinese merchants were there, Puk Foo Jang, Sang Chong Loong, Sang Chong Wah, Hook Wah Jang – Chinese wholesalers. And the Chinese had these gambling games, Fan Tan and Pakka Pu. It was illegal but they didn't stop it. And us kids would go down, 'buying rice' we called it, because you can't win! You're just 'buying rice' for a Chinaman.

Fan Tan was a piece of oil-cloth, with a cross on it, on the table under a dirty old lamp. There was no electric lights. You could hardly see the bloody thing. And there was one, two, three, four marked on the cross, see. Well, If you fancied the One you put your sixpence on it. Put it on the Number One square. That was the one you wanted to win. Well, if Number One came up, he'd pay you double money with the money back. If you put a trey-bit, threepence, on, you'd get a zack, sixpence, and your tray, back. If you wanted to go Nim, that was between One and Two, you put your threepence on the line, and if it come One or Two, you'd get your money back. Just even money, see.

Queensland Meat Export Company Meatworks at Ross River, 1917.

He'd have a saucer, and he'd fill it with Chinese coins or shells, and he put it on the table. This is long before the game starts. And then you back what you want. Then he'd take a chop stick and he'd pull four away. Puts them on the side. And what ever was left, one, two, three, four, was what won the set. But I could never get round the outside of it. He always got me! But that's what you did just for the hell of it.

And Pakka Pu was what you say, like the Pools. There was a ticket and there was a line across and there was a hundred marks. And Chinese figure there, and another hundred there. Well, you go in the Chinaman's shop, and you mark a ticket. You might get a hundred pounds! Well, you get your ticket and you mark one there, and one there, and one there, you see, and you mark ten. And then he copies that and gives you a receipt as you might say, and gives you that back. He signs his name on it. Well, then when they draw the bank, which is drawn out of a hat, you might only get one. For one you get nothing. Two you get sixpence. For three you get a shilling. Now if you get ten marks, you break the bank, which is nearly impossible. But if you broke the bank you got a hundred pounds. And my word the copper would boot your backside if you get caught! It's illegal but they can't stop 'em. They take a Chinaman to court today and there's another one starting up somewhere else tomorrow!

Flinders Lane was all little humpies. Harlots. But they were good people. They were dressed up nicely. They never abused anybody. And they never recognized a man they were with the night before! Behind Page's in the main part of the lane, there'd be five or six houses, little old places from the early days – where the parking station is now. The girls was mostly white but then there was Malay girls and a Chinee. And if you asked a girl, 'What are you doing this for?' she'd say, 'Well, I'm doing it for the money!' A lot of them had a couple of kids! And after a while they'd give it away and get married and they'd be a respectable married woman after that. Nobody knew.

'Boomerang Bend' up Denham Street below the Church of England was all overhanging trees. They'd go up there and do the act standing up for two bob. Katy Kelly was a well known prostitute. She had one of these stretchers that used to fold up into a square swag. Well, she had that and she used to put it up in the pub yard, near the wood heap, anywhere. She'd catch her customers on the way to the lavatory! You'd just walk past and take no notice of it. It's no use standing gawping. Somebody'd belt you! But I was never round the pubs that much. I didn't drink. Never drank and never smoked.

And they called getting an abortion 'rabbit catching'. There was some old tart that done it and the girl died. It was all kept quiet but we knew. So then if a fellow wanted to get a bit of 'rabbit catching' done, the sheila would get an address in Brisbane. And one of the young fellows on my shift got caught. He was playing around with a sheila and she said, 'Look, I'm 'that way' now! What are you going to do about it?

And he said, "Well, I dunno."

And she said, 'Well, you give me forty pound and I'm going to Brisbane.' The boat fare down was maybe seven pound. There was no train. Only coastal boats.

And he give her forty quid, and forty quid was best part of half a year's pay for him, but you had to do it if you wanted to get the girl out of the way. Borrow it and pay it back! And later on someone seen her down there and he said, 'Did you have the kid yet?'

'What kid!' she said. She'd took the forty quid and just buggered off!

All that was part of the town. The men laid it on the line to me; 'Don't go messing around with a good girl'.

And old Seymour, Detective Sergeant Seymour, he was a big fellow! Always wore a grey suit and a hard-hitter.[22] A very big man, six foot or more. He used to hunt us kids out of the Lane. Didn't stop us, but! You did these things! And Jimmy Dennis and I we went down to have a look, and he cops us and he said, 'What the hell are you doing down here! You young buggers! Get out!'

And we're telling him, 'We're only lookin!' And he's got Jimmy and me and he bangs our heads together! And I've had a sore head all me life, I reckon, from that! He nearly broke our skulls! But he wasn't always there and we used to go down.

And Show Time was a good chance to spend your money. There'd be all these tent shows, singing and dancing. *The Runaway Girl* and *After the Girl*. Good sort of plays. The Theatre Royal would be booked out, and the Olympia and the Stanley. That was all the theatres we had, so the rest would have to go in tents. Back of Pages. They used to go anywhere. Just put a tent on a paddock. No conveniences or nothing. If you wanted to pee you just went outside somewhere in the dark. They'd have a full cast and everybody did something. Even the leading lady would have to give a hand to put the tent up. They

---

22   Derby hat.

didn't have much. The girls would cook the stew inside the tent. And then they were all cleaned up before the show started.

And circuses, they'd come.[23] The Kalino Brothers were high-wire walkers, but the tent was only low. So they rigged this wire about fifteen feet off the ground on wire-hawsers and springs. There's no electric light. They had kerosene lamps, which was like a tank and a pipe and a cluster which lighted with a white light. And this Kalino'd get on this wire with his slippers and he did his act. Well, then interval came. And my mate, Jimmy and me, we're sitting there and I said, 'I betcha I could walk that bloody wire!'

And he said, 'Betcha couldn't!'

And I said, 'Betcha I could!'

And he said, 'Well, get out and walk it!'

And I said, 'Well, you come out too!' So we go out. And it's interval and the crowd's eating their lollies and peanuts. And I climb this bit of a ladder. And I get hold of this thing at the back and I'm going to just walk out a bit and run back. And I'm doing a bit of an act and Kalino comes out! The Wire-walker! And I'm thinking, 'Oh! Cripes! He'll kick my backside!'

But he says, 'Would you lika to walka the wire?' And I says, 'Yeah!'

'Well, Come on!' he says. And he get up, and the crowd's watching now, and he gets my two hands and he walks backwards, and he says, 'You looka to me! You donah look down!' And I walked the bloody wire! The crowd give me a

---

23   (Townsville 1770 and After, Vol 3; Townsville Museum Inc.). Rather incredibly, considering that the only means of transport were coastal boats, circuses had been coming to Townsville since the 1880s. In 1885 Mathews' Circus brought the first elephant seen in Townsville.

good clap. See, everyone knew me. They thought it was part of the act!

And then they bring on this Shetland Pony. And they say, 'Can any boy ride this pony?' And the boys'd get on and the pony would give a bit of a buck and a shake and get rid of them. And I won't have anything to do with horses. I hate the bloody things. But Jimmy says, 'I'll ride that bastard!' So he goes out.

And the clown says, 'Can you ride?'

And Jimmy say, 'Yes! Of course I can ride!' So he gets on this little horse, and he could nearly touch the ground. And he locks his two legs under the horse's forelegs. And he's thinking, 'I'll make sure the bugger doesn't get me off!' And he's holding the reins, all ready!

And the clown says to the little horse, 'Now you've got this fellow on your back. Do you think you can get rid of him?' And the horse never went one step! Just bends his knees, and drops! Jimmy goes straight over his head! Talk about laugh! Nearly brought the tent down!

Oh! Yes! Tent Shows! They was good! Whatever was on in town you went and seen it. You made your own excitement!

† NEWMAN

The Apprentice – 1914-1918

'I Learned to Love the Game'

In 1915 everybody was poor. I worked in different jobs, the best you could do. And my mother decided that I must be a tradesman.

And Mum said, 'You've got to learn a trade.'

And I said, 'No, I'm doing all right.' I was getting good money at the meatworks.

But she put the kibosh on this. She says, 'We're going to get you apprenticed, Joe.'

And I says, 'Where?'

And she says, 'The Railway!' And the railway didn't pay full money, you know. I didn't want to work there. They always paid less money than outside to a tradesman. Not that I cared much in them times.

Anyway, Mum's about four foot nothing in high heels, and we go to Bob Neals, he was the Chief Engineer. And we go to his office and he says, 'Yes, lady, what do you want?'

And she says, 'I want my son to be a tradesman.'

And he says, 'Hummph. What's your education?' And I'm buggered. I've had none, see!

But I says, 'Oh, pretty fair!'

And he says, 'Did you finish school?' I says, 'No, Me father died. I've bin working since I was twelve.'

'That's bad,' he says. So he says, 'What do you want to be?' I says, 'I want to be an engineer!' And he said, 'All right.'

And it turns out that the Chief Clerk, Mick Moynihan, he had a nephew named Copper Flaherty, and he's trying to work Copper in.

A cattle train from the west bringing cattle in Ross River or Alligator Creek meatworks. The "cow-catcher" at the front of the engine was a standard feature of Queensland trains.

And he did work Copper in, and he gets in the Engineering Shop because he was sort of related. And so Bob Neal, the Chief Engineer said, 'Will you go in the Blacksmith's Shop?'

And I wanted to be an engineer. But I said, 'Yeah. Till I can get a job in the Fitting Shop.'

'I'll put you in the Blacksmith's Shop until Fitting's ready,' he says. Of course, that's hopeless! You never get out.

'Righto!' I says. So Copper gets into the good shop and I get the fish shop! And I couldn't get out of that so I was signed up and had to stay there till I served my time.

Your mother was a hero for getting you to serve your time. You were lucky in a mother that did without things to get you there. See, I was working at the meatworks and I'd of got more money. My mother did without all of that to get me a tradesman.

She has to make a sacrifice in doing it, because when you're serving your time – which is Australian – in the Old Country 'serving your time' was like coming out of gaol! – you were serving your apprenticeship. You only got 7/6 a week – that's seventy-five cents. Well, normally, you would be labouring somewhere for fifteen bob a week, or something like that. You could get that down town working in the sawmill or anywhere you like. And you're coming up and you're making a fair sort of a wage. Well, your mother had to sacrifice to make you a tradesman, see. You weren't bringing home as much money, see. You've got to admire her!

We were poor but we was all tradesmen. I had two brothers and one sister. My sister was in a tailor's shop. She come up a tailoress. And my brother was in a painter's shop. My father was a tailor. He had a job to go to at Hillman's the Tailors and he started there directly we came out. I was twelve when he died and he was forty-two. And my young brother went to school. He died soon, with sugar.

THE LATEST IN TAILORING.

Mr J. HINDMARSH, MANAGER

GLOBE TAILORING COMPANY has once more got into HARNESS. He has bought the LATEST for SUMMER SUITINGS and the GLOBE STOCK is WORTH INSPECTING.

NEXT WEEK ANOTHER LARGE SHIPMENT WILL ARRIVE.

To meet the most fastidious the best place for SUITS

The Globe Tailoring Coy
Flinders-street, Townsville.

Before, the employers were ruthless! They'd put you on for five years, and then told yer, ' Oh, Joe...!' And he'd have a row with you. And you've got nothing! No papers! And then another blacksmith shop, they'll say 'Give you a job, Joe!'... but, 'You work two years for me "For improvement" and I'll give you your ticket!' And he gets two years sweat outa you! He's got you sweating two years on a boy's rates! And I'm a Tradesman! And eventually he'll give me my papers, see. Otherwise I'm nothing!

Even the railway used to shove 'em off at five years. Oh, it was common! A lot of men were tradesmen but never got their ticket, see. And when I eventually got them papers, Oh, it's 'Don't lose them!' Anyhow, they decide that they're gonna find what education you got. And I had nothing! I had none! So we go down the back-store and a chief clerk, a man named Mr. Healyan. He's got a black-board there, and he writes figures on the black-board and you gotta add 'em up quick and write the answer down on your paper, see. Well, I wasn't any good in mathematics. Pretty good at everything else! But not that! Anyhow, we goes through all this for us boys in the back-store, and these other kids, they had education and they could write them down, see. Anyhow, Joe's a glorious last! I'm the dunce!

Anyhow, Joe King was our foreman. And I'm last. I didn't care! I was never afraid of 'I'll get outa this!' sort of thing! Confidence from working. And I go back, I tell Joe King I failed, see. And I said, 'Well, Mr. King,' I said, 'I... I run last!' And I said, 'Don't forget! Somebody had to be last!'

And he says, 'Yes, Joe. There's always got to be a last horse in the race.'

And I said, 'Well, now, do I get the sack, or what?'

'No,' he said, 'You go down the blacksmith's shop. You'll make a good blacksmith. It doesn't matter so much about education, as long as you can forge steel, and sweat and live in the heat. You'll get your education as you go.' So I went back and I'm duly signed on, then, see. My step-father had to counter-sign the papers because he was responsible to make you obey, see.

Anyhow, then, of course, you served your time, and the wages gradually went up. And the boilermakers' boys, Joe and

Paddy, reckoned they weren't getting enough money. They're working hard, same as I am. And they go to old Bob Neal and he says, 'I'll give you another shilling a week!' So Joe and Paddy go down for another shilling in the book. So I didn't waste time! I went straight down the office. 'You give them another shilling! I want a shilling! I work as hard as they do!' And I'm brow-beating Bob Neal. And in the end he laughed and he give me the shilling. But he said, 'No more of that! Don't you try that on me again!'

Normally you'd only get your increase at the end of a year. Only then. For five years. But we knew more in five than they'd know in fifty today! See, I can do anything!

We were making pumpers for the two-foot gauge, for the cane-fields up north. A pumper is, there was a seat, and another seat, and you both pull. Your feet was on the pedal, and when you pull back, you pushed it, and when I pushed it would come my way. You pull the lever towards you and it works a bloody big gear which is off a pattern off a lathe. We made them for the cane-fields.

Really, in them places, there was no roads then, all boggy, and the women in them areas came to town with them and did their shopping. It was a two-foot gauge line for the sugar industry, but the public used it, with a pump-trolley. If a train come along you'd pull the trolley off the line, and then put it back. Of course, there was handles on the four corners. It was a bit of a lift, but you could lift it. You take hold of the handles and lift it off. It'd be three hundred-weight. And you could carry all your stuff on the seat with you. The women took 'em to town. You'd have to watch for the cane-loco, but he could see you before you seen him.

And in the Railway yards, when we had our dinner-break, there'd be goats come from everywhere. In them days there were wild goats up the hill. Hundreds of the buggers. And, oh, they was cunning! Before dinner there wouldn't be a goat in the railway yard, just before the twelve o'clock whistle blew and we'd start throwing the crusts about, the goats, straight from the hill! There wouldn't be a crust or a bit of paper left for the flies to get on! And before the one o'clock whistle, they're straight back up the hill! They knew!

And one time there, I get a bit of steel in my eye. Nothin' will get it out, swabs, nothin'! And this Abo. bloke says, 'I git it out, Joe.' And it's hurting to buggery. I'll try anything! And he gets his tongue and licks it across my eye and the steel come out, and I didn't even feel it! They had their own ways, see, and good ways, too. I coulda done without his oniony breath, but!

Anyhow, the five years are coming up. Then you get scared. You got to have a test job. No money if you don't pass the test job. Well, you don't know what the test job is and nobody's going to tell you. They spring it on you and make you fail. See, they don't want you getting higher money!

And this Copper Flaherty that got in the machine-shop – dumb as an ox – he's lined up for his test job. Those slide bars that the piston works on, well, they're to be set to a piano-wire! They got to be set right. And the locomotive's in the middle of the shop – nobody goes near you when you're on your test job! No-one can't say, 'What's that going on outside?' or so on. It's not done! If the trademan's on the bench over here and yells out 'Copper!' and the boss comes along, it's 'You shut your mouth!' Because he's got to go through it alone! This is his test.

So poor old Copper, he couldn't straighten ... see, the wire comes through the cylinder and to the crank on the locomotive wheel and then he sets... see, that's true centre ... then he sets his guide-bars that the thing slides on to this piano-wire. Which is quite a job. And a hard case named Dick Tate was on the bench. And Copper sings out, 'Hey! Dick! This bloody thing don't line up!'

And Dick calls back, 'Pull the wire!'

You pull the piano-wire tight to get it straight, see. And Copper says, 'I broke it once! There's something wrong!' Well, Copper never had his guide-bars set, see.

So, Dick, clown as he was, said, 'Go up and get the master straight-edge[24] Now, this is a beautiful thing about nine foot long, nickel-plated. Made in Scotland. The bloody best, you know!

So Copper goes up, and Martin Fife, he's in what we the Monkey's Arse, it's a wire-netting house; he's the tool-man. He gives you everything out. And Copper goes up and he wants the master straight-edge. Well, it never goes out! You took your straight-edge up and you put it against it but you never got the master straight-edge out! But he gets it!

And he comes down, and then he puts it on his wire and

---

24   Although Joe uses this term six times throughout this anecdote, never once was his enunciation clear enough to be certain that 'Straight-edge' was what he was saying. As it was a technical term the Interviewer should perhaps have asked him to repeat it so that a layperson could clearly understand what was being said, for example, by saying. Would you mind just explaining a little about this 'straight-edge' – am I saying that correctly?'

then he puts it on the other where he's trying to level up, – and Dick's not supposed to come near him, see – and Dick's working on the bench. But the boss wasn't about. 'Hey! Dick!' Copper says, 'There's something not true!'

Coal-loaded facilities operated by compressed air, Townsville Railway yards, about 1920.

And of course, Dick was a clown. And he says, 'The master straight-edge ain't true!' Well, it's impossible, see!'

So Copper says, 'What'll I do?'

Well, you've got to laugh, now! But Dick says, 'Oh, look, go up and get some emery paste and lap it in on the lathe.'

So Copper's got the master straight-edge, which shouldn't be touched, on the lathe-bed, and he's grinding it in! Ruining an absolutely bloody true thing!

And they catch him! Oh, Gawd! He got his arse kicked over that lot! They kicked your backside all right! It was the master straight-edge, and they'd paid a fortune for this flaming thing!

So Copper failed his test job. He was just washed out. Well, he's got to stop there another twelve months at the last rate. He don't get his ticket! Poor old Copper! Because he's not brainy enough to add things up.

Anyhow, I went to Joe King and I said, 'When am I getting my test job? 'Oh! You'll know!' he said.

I said, 'But I want to ask the men a lot. It's getting near my five years.' And I want my test job, because I want the tradesmen's money! I've worked here five years and I've done me good job.

Anyhow, we're building the two-foot-gauge railway for the sugar people, for sugar and passengers. The industry wanted the two-foot gauge, and I'm making up these carriage and wagon parts. And of course, the labourers take my finished work to the machine-shop to drill, and it gets all bent and comes back, and I'm playing hell about them spoiling my work. And it's coming back.

And in the end I come out of me Time, and I get tradesmens' rates, straight away. And I thought, 'Well now!' Mr. Hanlon, he was the Pay Clerk, he was responsible. And I get full rates. And I went to Hanlon, and I said, 'This is wrong! I'm not even a tradesman!'

And he says, 'Well, That's what they told me to give you, Joe. I'm not losing.'

So I go to Jack Cahil, the head clerk of the show, and he says, 'No, that's right, Joe. You're a tradesman!'

And I say, 'I haven't had me bloody test job!'

So I go to King, and I say, 'Look, Mr. King. I don't want to mess things up. I want the tradesmens' rate, but I haven't had a test job.'

'Oh, you had it! And you passed it!' he said.

'Oh, did I? What was it?' I says.

'Oh, all that stuff for the two-foot gauge,' he says. 'Remember when it used to come back all twist and broken! We tried to break it, you know! We tried to smash the lot and we couldn't. You didn't know !'

So I get me tradesmens' rate.

And old Joe King gave me the papers with quite a bit of ceremony. Old Joe liked me. He said, 'Now, Young Joe. There's your papers, and look after them A lot of people have to see them, you know, so keep'em clean. You'll have to show them.'

They were your proof. 'There's my papers, Mate!' You know. But I never had to show them because I could do the job. I was known. And three years poor old Copper Flaherty missed his test job. I wouldn't have stopped three years! And he never got his ticket and he's on boy's pay all the time. And blacksmiths got more that fitters, about a shilling, so I'm laughing!

And at this time it was during the Great War and I was in the A.G.C. on Kissing Point, which is Jezzine Barracks, now. Australian Gunnery Corps. Like Cadets. I would be seventeen or eighteen. And I hated it. I hated being regimented. Because I wasn't the type.

Anyhow, we're on guard duty all standing there. And this Staff Sergeant, or somebody, is showing us how to work a rifle, a .303. And he's yakking away. And he says, 'Well, stand easy.'

And I turn my rifle upside down in the sand, nozzle-down, and I lean on the butt. I hate the thing, see.

And he's yapping away and he turns round and he sees me; 'You stupid bastard!' he says.[25]

I says, 'Who?'

'You!' he says, 'Pick that rifle up!' And, Christ, I pick it up and all the sand runs down the barrel, see!

Oh, did he perform! He said, 'You're not worth trusting with a rifle! I'll give you something you can dig in the bloody dirt, Mate!' And he give this rifle to another boy to pull-through, to get this sand out. And, 'Come with me! I'll give you something you can dig in the bloody dirt!'

And he give me a long-handled shovel. And I had to dig the drain from the ablution block, which was the bathroom, to the salt-pan to get the water off the flat. And this suited me fine! This is better than soldiering! I'm shovelling dirt, and not giving a damn! Because I felt I was doing something. But to walk round with a gun, with nothing in it, and jump when he yells, was just not me. I was just a wash-out in the army!

I don't regiment. I do my own thinking! See, suppose you're telling a boy how to saw wood, and you say, 'Now, that's the right way. Your finger on the top of the saw, and you saw like that.'

And he says, 'What if you're left-handed?' Well, he's got you buggered, hasn't he! There's no 'right way' anywhere. I've always did me own thinking. I only believe in common sense, see. I didn't believe because they said so. I believe when I found out that it was worth believing in.

---

25   Nothing in the printed word can convey the sense of outraged wrath in the sergeant's voice as remembered and mimicked by Joe. It was something like 'You...oo Stuoooo...pid BAAAss.. stid!!

And I stayed in the railway working for £3.15 a week. I never drank and I never smoked so I always had a quid about me. And then I got a blacksmith's shop in Julia Creek. I wanted to be my own boss. I decided that if I was gonna be a blacksmith I might as well be a good one. And I learned to love the game. Anything to do with tools.

When I look back, it was a marvellous life. If I died tomorrow I'd say I had a good time today! And I wouldn't be crooked on one thing that happened. Because I caused half of the bloody things meself!

Part Two
Joe's Mates

Harry Pope

When I was about nine, I got tonsilitis. The doctor came down in his horse and sulky. If your family was in the Lodge, you had the Lodge doctor. Groups of workers, called a Lodge, would club together and put in maybe a couple of bob (about 50 cents) a week to help one another in hard times of sickness or death in a family. So I've got this tonsilitis, and the doctor came down and he said to Mother, 'If he's no better tomorrow when I come, I'll take them out.'

So, sure enough he comes, and they were no better. So he sat me in a chair in the doorway in the front of the house. And he put an instrument down me throat, like scissors. And he snipped one off. And I got up to walk away. And he said, 'Wait on! There's another one to come!' And I sat down and he took the other one out. No anaesthetic. He just told me to gargle with salt and water. And Mum paid the two bob.

We had a little house on low blocks and there was a bougainvillea all over the front verandah, very prickly. And m' father bought m' brother and me some wheels and we made a billy-goat cart. We had a lovely goat for it. Those goats, you'd see them going round the hill.

We used to take this cart out bush to get some wood in. We'd be out by about four o'clock in the morning and we'd be back by eight o'clock with a big load. And then we'd cut it up for the stove and for the boiler outside for the washing. The washing was all done in kerosene tins, no proper boiler. Kerosene for the lights at night came in tins, two in a wooden case. Eight bob a case (about $2) for four gallons. And those tins, you put a length of fencing-wire in for a handle and you've got a fair sort of bucket. And the cases were good pine timber and everyone made furniture out of them.

And when I left school I couldn't get into the railway. I was too small. So I was going round on the baker's cart. Later I got in with some wheelwrights. No apprenticeship. You worked for five years for them, and then they give you full money and you're in the game, a tradesman.

Henry Brown

There were thirteen in my family and they raised nine. The brother next to me, he died, but I couldn't tell you what of. There were twins in the family but they died early; about two; rheumatic fever, I think it was. The only thing they give you for colds was kerosene; a few drops on a teaspoon on sugar.

We had a place in Charlotte Street in Aitkenvale. None of those streets was named then. Dad built our place straight out of the ground, with ironbark; ant-bed floor. He put down a well but it was no good. After you went down a certain way there was clay. Us kids had to cart the water from down the road a bit. You had to hand-pump it. And there was two empty hogs-head barrels at the back door we had to fill for Mum. We had to get up in the morning - no boots - and in winter time you'd hear the grass crackling under your feet with frost.

There wouldn't have been more than thirty hours in the whole of Aitkenvale then. Where Pimlico High School is now, Charlie Armstrong had it leased to a Chinaman. It used to be all Chinamens' gardens then. And Garbutt's slaughter-yard was where Warina is now. From Hermit Park there was nothing here. Just a bush track and lantana. All lagoons and chinee apple.

And those Chinamens' gardens; they had everything; a kerosene-tin bucket of ripe tomatoes for sixpence; a cabbage, you'd get it for sixpence; lettuces; shallots; all your vegetables; pumpkins. And they'd always cut you a water-melon. You could eat as much water-melon as you liked, but don't take any away! And there were Chinamen used to go round the town with a stick on their shoulder with baskets on the ends. They sell you pineapples and lollies. And every year at Christmas they give you a Christmas Box; Chinese ginger, all done up in a blue jar.

Dad was strict. He might tell you to clean out a certain patch of weeds, and if you didn't have it done by the time he come back, well, Look Out! You had very little time for yourself. We never used to go anywhere. We might go down to the river for a swim, where the Nathan Street bridge is now. Or, in the floods, we'd walk way up the river and wait for a big old tree to come floating down and we'd swim out to it and come down on it. Or we'd swim out to a paper-bark branch and catch hold of it and have a spell, just hanging on. But the logs was the best!

I started work at twelve. I didn't know what it was to have a pair of boots on me feet till then. I was Spare Boy for Dad on his horse team. You stand around the horses and hook them up. And bring the spare horses along behind the team. Dad always had a dog, a blue dog. He never let anyone feed it; only himself. If the dog didn't do what he wanted it to, he'd get it with the butt of Dad's whip. We had a pretty hard life.

A horse team on the Georgetown road. Henry Brown had his first pair of boots when as a twelve-year-old he started work for his teamster father as 'spare boy'.

Julius Mathieson

My Dad was a battler. He started our farm out at Major's Creek. He made our house out of bush timber; all the furniture from kerosene cases.

There was eight of us in the family and where we all slept I just can't tell you. No shoes. We didn't know anything about shoes. But we never went short of food. Dad'd kill a beast and there was a vat and we'd have corned beef. We had chooks and they camped in the mulberry tree. We were close to the Serpentine Lagoon and Dad had his Snider so we had always had ducks. There was a covered-in lavatory down the back-yard with a corn sack for a door. For baths we swam in the creek.

Dad grew tomatoes, pumpkins, corn, sweet-potatoes. Any vegetables; fruit. He'd take it into town on the dray but sometimes there'd be no demand for whatever he had and they'd all be dumped. And he'd have to pay a dumping fee. And that could be a year's work! And there'd be droughts or floods. In the end he gave in and we moved into town and Dad got a job on the railway. I'd be about six or seven and I started school at West End.

Friday nights we'd walk into town. The shops'd all be open and Flinders Street would be crowded. We'd walk from the Post Office down to Lowth's and back again. Everybody would be there, meeting friends and shaking hands. And you'd have an ice-cream or a cold drink and away you'd go home. That was a good night out.

We'd swim at Sandy Crossing or we'd build little flatties and row down to the mouth of the river. My brother Jack never got any schooling out at Major's Creek but he was clever. He built a little twelve-footer and we took her over to Magnetic Island. We thought we were just it! We climbed up the hill and cut the top off a little pine tree to lash to the top of the mast to sail home. We were that proud of ourselves!

When I was about thirteen or fourteen I started work at Rooney's Mill; as floor-boy at first, sweeping up the sawdust. Joe Clarke was my mate. Joe's father had died and his Mother was pretty hard up. She was doing washing to keep the family going. If Joe didn't have any crib the men would get him to sing – he had a good voice and knew all the songs – and then they'd give him something from their own crib. My Mother would often as not put something extra in my crib-bag for him. Bread and dripping with salt and pepper was a favourite.

After a while I got a promotion to a bench, working with tools; mostly assembling doors and sashes. And you wouldn't believe the sailing ships coming up the river with big logs from Innisfail and Tully. They'd winch them up on to the wharf. We had this five-foot diameter saw and a saw called a breaking-down saw and another that would cut the log up into planks. And there were big timber-racks and trolleys. Rooney's supplied all the western districts.

And one time Old Man Rooney and Mrs. Rooney and their daughter Cecilia went down to Maryborough buying timber and they were coming back on the *Yongala*. On the way back the *Yongala* ran into a cyclone and she was lost with all hands; the Rooneys and all the Townsville people that were on board were all drowned. It was a terrible tragedy.

So I was at my trade at Rooney's until war broke out. There were three of us decided to enlist, Jack McShirring, myself and Mac McTagney. We arranged to meet at the barracks at North Ward but I was the only one that went. The others didn't turn up. Joe Clarke had given them an earful about how tough life in the army would be. He didn't want a bar of it and told them what mugs they'd be to have sergeants bawling at them all day. So they shied off.

My battalion went overseas on the *Arcadia* from Brisbane. We were on the front at Ypres and then we were transferred down to Pozieres. Oh! Pozieres was a battle alright! Those Prussian guards we were up against had these helmets with a coat-of-arms on the front and a spike on the top. After that battle the majority of our lot all had one of those helmets for a souvenir. But not me. I didn't want to remember what it had been like. All those dead lying out there like that. Just young blokes like us mostly. Ours too. Terrible!

At Polygon Wood I got a bit of shrapnel in my leg from a high explosive. The corporal told me to get back to the aid-post, and the Orderlies told me, 'In the wagon!' The doctor at the First Australian Hospital told me to count myself lucky I didn't lose my leg.

When it was all over there was the Victory March in London. We were all camped in Hyde Park in London and we marched past the front of Buckingham Palace. And there was the King! We thought we were made, being so close to the King. But then the trouble was we didn't want to go back to camp. We wanted leave! We all sat down. We wouldn't take orders. So the officers got together and they managed to get leave for the week-end for us. And weren't we happy!

I met a few North Queensland fellows over there; Talbot Heatley, and Inglis-Smith – he got killed, poor chap! – and Trotter and Arthur Doig. Him and me we were good mates. Anyone from Townsville or the Towers, we always stuck together.

The ruin of Pozières windmill. Australian troops fell more thickly on this ridge than any other battlefield of the war.

Florrie Toombs

Father was a drover out west and got hurt. He was sent to Townsville hospital. He was in for a good while. Mother had me, Hannah, the twins and Baby so she had to put Hannah and me in the orphanage. She took a cottage in Hale Street then she could get us out.

She went out washing. She had to pay the rent and keep us. She got six shillings a day and she finished about eight o'clock at night. Many a time I'd go down Wills Street to come home with her. She'd say, 'Oh! Florrie! Don't come down in the dark! You never know who might be about!' I'd say, 'I'm not frightened, Mum.' I used to go because she'd be that tired.

Hale Street wasn't much of a street then; just a bit of a track. We were not that far from where the Clarks lived; they were just across the street, up the hill a bit. Joe was working at Rooney's Mill but I was still at school so he seemed a bit more grown up. He'd come over some Saturdays and chop a bit of firewood for Mum.

Where the Cutting is now we used to go chasing goats up the hill. Joe'd get up on a rock and sing for all the world to hear. He had a good voice. And he was good at chasing goats. If we caught a little kiddie-goat people would pay five shillings for them. That was good money in them days.

When it rained, there used to be a water-fall come down

off Castle Hill into a big gully through Wills Street and Walker Street with big waterholes along it. We used to swim in them.

I'd have loved to have been a nurse but I didn't have the education. I left school at thirteen. Mother had a boarding-house by then, over in Davidson Street; mainly for the wharf-lumpers. She'd give them their breakfast and the tea at night; rissoles and sausages; nothing fancy. There was a big shed out the back where they slep'.

I used to wait on the tables, and this morning I said to one of them, 'You didn't come in for your tea last night.' 'No', he said, 'The boat didn't come in' It was the *Yongala*. There was a cyclone, and she'd sunk off the Cape. Some of the Rooneys was on it. Nurse Rooney and one of her brothers. And some Nurses that had gone down to do their exams. A lot of Townsville people were on it. They never found any bodies. Only a race-horse washed up dead on the Cape.

Townsville Ovrphanage, North ward, 1909

John Walker

You didn t bother much about shoes in those days. We'd go out in the morning to get the cows in and you'd stub your toe on a piece of hard manure, in the early morning. Awhh! Gee! You'd think your foot was coming off!

At home we had carbide lamps that were like two cylinders. The water was on the outside and the carbide was on the inside, and the water used to drip very slowly. They gave a good light, too, but sometimes the carbide would cut out and you would be just in the middle of something and you're in the dark. You'd have to go outside and start it all over again.

And I got a job in Townsville. I was boarding in Mitchell Street in North Ward, boarding with a mate. His mother owned the house. I used to walk to work over the hill. There was a little shop and I'd buy a packet of biscuits on the way and that would be my dinner. At week-ends me and my mate, Joe, we'd go chasing billy-goats round the hill, or pinching a few guavas from the back of the Chinese gardens.

Townsville was pretty primitive then. Flinders Street was just a succession of potholes full of mud. And in the wet season they'd go 'Swisht! Swisht!' on to the footpaths. Public transport was horse-buses. And the driver, he'd have a long whip, and he'd whip behind to catch any boys sneaking a free ride at the back. The mail ship was the *Bingera*. She was a steam turbine. Every Monday morning, regular as clockwork, you'd see her coming in.

Bikes were scarce. I bought a bike on time payment, half a crown (25 cents) a week. I used to ride that bike in to work. I had a carbide light for it All you needed was a dozen little lumps of carbide about the size of your fingernail. And you turn the water on and away she went.There were very few cars about. The first car I remember seeing in Townsville was a French car owned by a doctor.

And I did some training in the Militia in the Light Horse and the Artillery. We used to have a camp at Easter at Kissing Point. Joe was in it, too, but he was a bit of a dud. Not his game. When the war came I served in France with the Infantry.

Appendix

(1) List of passengers arriving on the *Limerick*

Port of *Townsville* (INWARDS). Queensland.

A List of Crew and Passengers that have arrived in the S.S. *Limerick from London*

LIST OF CREW.

Paper Articles

LIST OF PASSENGERS.

ADULTS.					CHILDREN.	
Above 12 Years of Age.					Under 12 Years of Age.	
Males.	Females.		Males.	Females.	Males.	Females.

INFANTS.

Under 1 Year of Age.

Males.	Females.

SUMMARY.

						TOTAL.
18		13		1	2	43

Customs House, *Townsville*

(2) Immigration Nominee Form: Clark Family

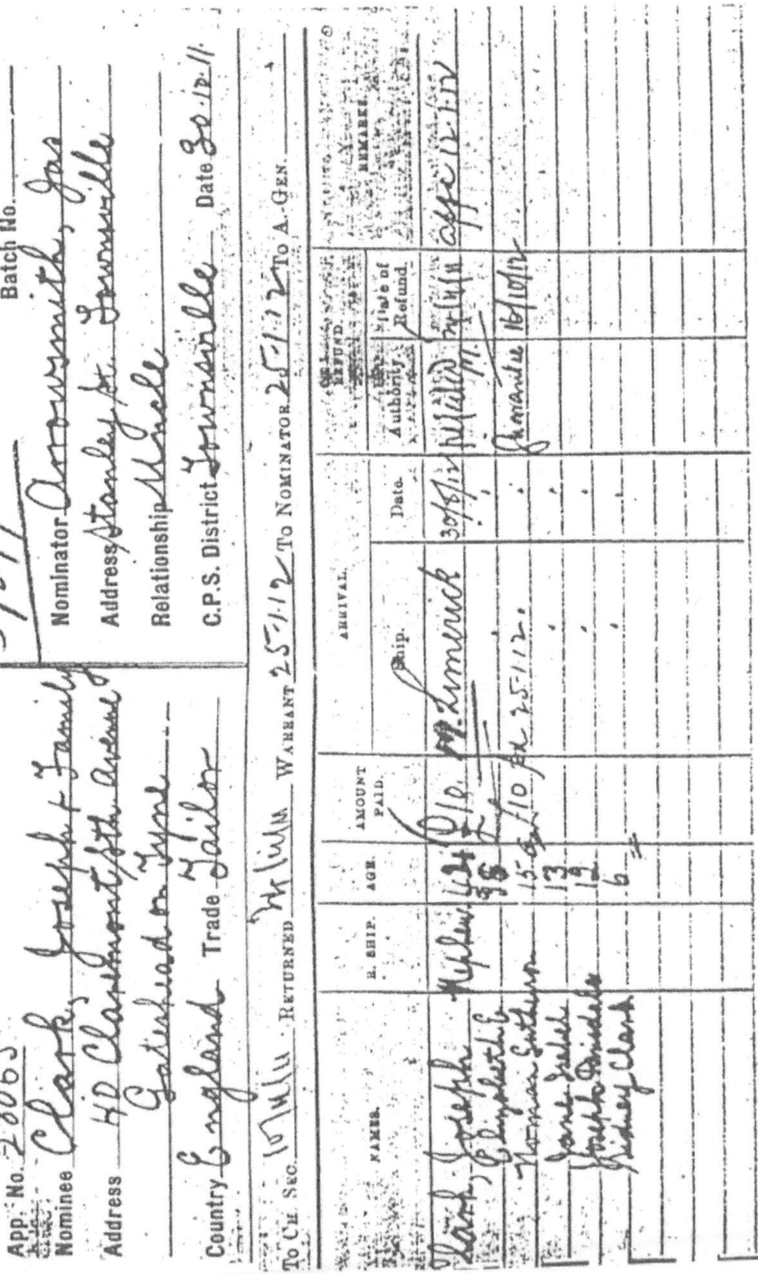

(3) Extract from Townsville Electoral Roll, 1915, showing 864, Elizabeth Eleanor Clark, Stanley Street.

851......Christensen, William, Stagpole St., labourer, 21 Sep., 1910, M

852 ......Christensen, Patrick, Mitchell St., public servant, 2 Oct., 1911, M

853 ......Christensen, Susan Stewart, Mitchell St., housewife. 2 Oct., 1911, F

854 ......Christian, Leila Isabel, Subdeanery, Townsville, domestic duties, 5 Aug., 1914, F

855 ......Church, Doreas Naomi, Townsville Orphanage, submatron, 1 June, 1907, F

856 ......Claffey, Mary, Strand, housewife, 2 April, 1914, F

857 ......Claffey, Patrick Joseph, Strand, teamster, 2 April, 1911, M

858 ......Clancy, Eliza Marie, Sturt St., housewife, 8 Aug., 1905, F

859 ......Clancy, Ellen, Supreme Court, housewife, 8 Aug., 1905, F

860 ......Clancy, John Joseph, Sturt st., coachbuilder, 12 May, 1909, M

861......Clancy, Patrick Thomas, Cleveland Ter, next Supreme Court, messenger, 31 May,

1901, M

862 ......Clancy, Thomas. Flinders St.. labourer, 5 April, 1898, M

863 ......Clark, Cyril, Flinders St., chainman, 23 May, 1912, M

864 ......Clark, Elizabeth Eleanor, Stanley St., domestic duties, 4 Aug., 1914, F

865 ......Clark, Hannah, Wills st. West, housewife. 14 July, 1905. F

866 ......Clark, James. Hale St., lorry driver, 28 July, 1913. M

867 ......Clark, John, Hale St., labourer, 28 July, 1913, M

868 ......Clark, John Somers, Trembath's, Morris St., 23 Feb., 1914, M

869 ......Clark, Lionel Bury, Union Bank, Flinders St., bank clerk, 29 Sep., 1905, M

870 ......Clark, Robert John, Union Bank of Australia. Limited, clerk, 3 April, 1914, M

871......*Clark, Thomas, Wills st. West, labourer, 1 April, 1903, M*

872......*Clark, Thomas James, Wills st. West, labourer, 8 Feb., 1907, M*

873......*Clarke, Arthur Cecil, Mitchell st., cycle mechanic, 3 Feb., 1911, M*

874......*Clarke, Fanny, Wills St., housewife, 2 Oct., 1911, F*

875......*Clarke, Firman, Wills St., allot. 2, sec. 68. picture frame maker, 2 Aug., 1905, M*

876......*Clarke, Frances, Mitchell St., housewife, 4 Feb., 1914, F*

877......*Clarke, Frances, Wills St., domestic duties, 6 May, 1911, F*

873......*Clarke, George Francis, Mitchell St., joiner, 3 Feb., 1911, M*

879......*Clarke, Gwendoline Annie, Mitchell St., housewife. 3 Feb., 1914, F*

880......*Clarke, Hugh Thomas, Mitchell St., labourer, 1 Feb., 1911, M*

881......*Clarke, Hugh Thomas, Cook St., hairdresser, 2 Dec. 1913, M*

882......*Clarke, Joseph, Flinders St., trainer, 6 Feb., 1912, M*

883......*Clarke, Mary Linda, Wills St., dressmaker, 17 Feb., 1908, F*

884......*Clarke, Stanton Smith, Wills St., bank messenger, 6 May, 1914, M*

885......*Clarke, William James, Taylor's Hotel, engineer, 11 Sep , 1913, M*

886......*Clarkson, Alice May, Alexandra St., domestic duties, 6 Oct., 1913, F*

(4) Extract from Clark Family Bible.

Grand parents   Copied from Family Bible

Joseph Clark   born   Aug. 22   1840   died   15 Oct 1914
Jane Gutherson   "   March 13   1833   "   31st March 1921
married   May 22nd   1865 } at   Stella
                                Co. Durham

John   born   March 7th   1866
Joseph   "   April 3rd   1867   died Dec 16/1912
Thomas   "   February 21   1869 • Oct 11 1933
Mary   "   June 26   1870 " Jan 9 1924
Jane   "   May 23   1872 "
William   '   July 22   1874 " May 29 /35
Robert   '   March 8   1876 , June 19 '57

all   born   at   Close House , Wylam
as was Grandfather .   Northumberland

(5) Extracts from the *North Queensland Register*, April 1911

The Loss of the *Yongala*

The *Yongala* wreckage found at Palm Island

Hand coloured postcard of S.S. Yongala, ca. 1905.
State Library of Queensland

April 9, 1911. A resident who has spent the last fortnight at Palm Islands and who returned last night, has afforded a representative of the *Northern Miner* the following interesting information as to the wreckage found on Palm Islands and which has been noticed there since Sunday March 26th.

Mr Butler, the lessee of Great Palms, and the guests of his pleasure resort first noticed wreckage coming up on Sunday March 26th, when they discovered three tins of kerosene bearing the mark 'Tidewater' Oil on the south side of Great Palm. Next day they made a more systematic search and picked up small pieces of freshly painted and newly broken boards, among which was a fair quantity of some dark dressed timbers, cedar or teak, and which had been varnished. Some of these bore the figures '736' in conjunction with the words 'Officer Room', 'Pantry' or 'First Saloon – Smoking'.

For the next few days the weather was very rough and wet and nothing could be done. On Thursday March 30th, a further search was made. Esk Island was examined and there were found a half-grating from N°. 5 forehold which they gave to the captain of the *Kuranda*. At this island they also picked up a red plush cushion. It was a cushion which would be expected to be found in a first-saloon cabin and a remarkable feature about it was its most abominable stench. The cushion was opened and found to be stuffed with feathers and there was nothing in the contents to account for the odour. On Sunday notwithstanding rain, another party went over and again examined the north sitde of Great Palm. They picked up further wreckage with nothing to identify it except occasionally the figure '733'. Another party found apparently what had formed part of a settee in the second-saloon. They also found what looked like a piece of the taffrail and a rather large boat's mast, marked '4', and rigged, on Orpheus Island.

On Thursday last Mr Butler and two well-known amateur beachcombers made a thorough investigation of Eclipse Island and found on the lee side a seaman's chest painted very dark green and broken open. Near it was a canvas-covered lid and between the two was scattered a considerable quantity of clothing, notably a dark-blue top-coat of good quality, a white mess-jacket but no papers or any marks of identification except an handkerchief bearing the initials 'R.D.G.'

Bibliography

Historical Background

Blainey, Geoffrey; *A Land Half Won*; Griffin Press; Adelaide; 1980

Gibson-Wilde, Dorothy; *Gateway to a Golden Land, Townsville to 1884*; James Cook University; Townsville; 1994.

Gibson-Wilde, Dorothy; *A Pattern of Pubs; Hotels of Townsville 1864 - 1914*; James Cook University; Townsville; 1988

Gibson-Wilde, Dorothy and Dalton, B.J; *Townsville 1888*; James Cook University; Townsville; 1990

Macintyre, Stuart; *The Oxford History of Australia, Vol 4*; M.U.P; 1993

Mathew, John; *Townsville 1770 and After*, Townsville Museum Incorporated; 1996

Oral History

Caunce, Steven; *Oral History and the Local Historian*; Longman; London; 1994

Frisch, Michael; *A Shared Authority. Essays on the Craft and Meaning of Oral and Public History*; State University of New York Press; 1990

Humphries, Steve; Mack, Joanna; and Perks, Robert; *A Century of Childhood*; Sidgwick and Jackson; London; 1989

Lummis, Trevor; *Listening to History*.

Perks, Robert; *Oral History, Talking about the Past*; Oral History Society; London; 1988

Thomson, Alistair; *Anzac Memories, Living With the Legend*; M.U.P; Melbourne; 1994

Thompson, Paul; *The Voice of the Past*; O.U.P.; Oxford; 1988

Thompson, Thea; *Edwardian Children*; Routledge and Kegan Paul; London; 1981

Yow, Valerie; Recording Oral History; Sage; Thousand Oaks; 1994

Methodology

Standford, Michael; A Companion to the Study of History; Blackwell; Oxford; 1994

Books by
Marion Houldsworth

The Morning Side of the Hill

Barefoot Through The Bindies

Red Dust Rising

From Gulf to God Knows Where

Maybe It'll Rain Tomorrow

The Immigrant Boy